**Kris Gethin** is the director of trainers for Physique Global, who transformed Bollywood stars such as Hrithik Roshan, John Abraham, Mahesh Babu, Ranveer Singh, Arjun Kapoor and Karan Johar. He is the author of various books and graphic novels like *Bollywood Body by Design* and *Kaged Muscle*. He has certified over 1,800 trainers worldwide in the training principle, he founded, called DTP (Dramatic Transformation Principle). He is the CEO of KAGED MUSCLE Supplements which became the highest-rated brand in the world after only seven months of its launch. He is the spokesperson of the largest fitness website in the world—*www.Bodybuilding.com*—and has hosted the most-watched transformation video series on the web by attaining over 100 million viewers. He is a Natural Pro Bodybuilder and has secured second place in the Natural World Championships. He lives in Boise, Idaho and Wales, UK when he is not travelling the world hosting motivational seminars for Physique Global.

D1500059

The Transformer

Kris Gethin

Foreword
Anil Kapoor

Om Books International

First published in 2016 by

Om Books International

Corporate & Editorial Office
A-12, Sector 64, Noida 201 301
Uttar Pradesh, India
Phone: +91 120 477 4100
Email: editorial@ombooks.com
Website: www.ombooksinternational.com

Sales Office
107, Ansari Road, Darya Ganj,
New Delhi 110 002, India
Phone: +91 11 4000 9000, 2326 3363, 2326 5303
Fax: +91 11 2327 8091
Email: sales@ombooks.com
Website: www.ombooks.com

ISBN: 978-93-84225-68-1

Printed in India

10 9 8 7 6 5 4 3 2 1

Contents

Foreword

Healthy living is not a fad, it is a necessity; self-discipline is not about sacrificing all things good, it is a precursor to an enviable lifestyle. Kris Gethin's memoir, *The Transformer*, is an essential read for all those who aspire to achieve phenomenal physiques, not just to land on the cover of a leading fashion magazine, but to recognise the wonders of living and enjoying life sans health risks and fitness-related issues.

The trajectory that this memoir follows is interesting: from growing up with a loving family in Wales, feeling the rush of wheels in motocross at the age of six, going through the first of a series of physical transformations in Pontypridd, stepping into the shoes of a writer and photographer for *FLEX* magazine in the US and hobnobbing with the stalwarts of the bodybuilding world, to setting up a gym of his own in Sydney—Kris has worn several hats and played each role with passion and dedication.

Through his journey as a bodybuilder, Kris motivates his readers to avoid deadly perils such as inactivity and lack of regular exercise. Bollywood, for instance, is a world where it is very easy to fall into the trap of endless parties. I have always maintained a safe distance from such unnecessary indulgences. As an actor, I cannot compromise on my health; I need adequate amount of sleep so as to turn up at the next day's shoot in perfect shape. Seldom do I allow myself to let in a few cheat days in my diet routine.

In his memoir, Kris writes about overcoming such weaknesses while being on a luxury cruise line as an appointed fitness trainer. I particularly appreciated how Kris held himself back from eating popcorn at a movie theatre because he had spotted someone he'd trained and didn't want to let him down by setting a wrong example. Like Kris, I too have battled my cravings in order to be in the good books of my fans. The way Kris recounts how he overcame innumerable failures is commendable. The trick is not to let any defeat crush you; but to take the leap at the most opportune time.

Kris has never missed a meal in the last sixteen years and that goes to prove how vital it is to take care of our eating habits. For actors like us, who are always on the go, it gets difficult to accommodate all meals within requisite time frames. Kris's approach to health and fitness is not restricted to building muscles; he wants his readers to adopt a holistic perspective toward keeping fit and staying healthy.

The Transformer conveys the message of cultivating a positive attitude, setting right priorities and knowing more about preventing health hazards. 'Do what you fear and don't fear what you do' is Kris's mantra and that's how any transformation in any human being's life is possible. *The Transformer* can be anybody's story, anybody who is ready to get up and rise each time there's a fall, a stumble, a broken bone or a muscle tear. With Kris as your motivational mentor, learn to transform your career, health and spirit.

Anil Kapoor

1

A Hard Fall: Part I

When I stepped into Stacey McCulloch's office in September 2010, I was certainly curious but not prepared in the slightest for the news I was about to hear. My mind drifted to what seemed like more important thoughts about the Mr. Olympia contest I was due to attend in a matter of hours.

In the fifteen years since I first took control of my life, I had faced countless challenges. Each one had been bigger and harder than the last. As the confidence rooted in my transformation had grown, I never expected to come across a fight that would catch me completely off guard.

For the first time in my life I was entirely at peace with my surroundings. I had travelled the length and breadth of the earth in my work as a fitness trainer, masseur, professional bodybuilder and journalist. But in Boise, Idaho, I had met my match.

Boise, for those who don't know, is the capital of Idaho, situated in the foothills of the Rocky Mountains in the United States of America; a stunning, if relatively, small city with all the charm of North-West America. Its summers are hot and its winters are cold. It's an honest place with honest, hard-working people.

It's also home to Bodybuilding.com, which was how I was lucky enough to cross paths with it. Three years previously,

Ryan Deluca, CEO of Bodybuilding.com had invited me to become Editor-in-Chief of the website, a role that I had thrived in and thoroughly enjoyed.

The work was fulfilling and I was satisfied with the way my life was shaping up. You don't expect to have the rug pulled out from beneath you when everything is set just right. But that's the moment when you are at your most vulnerable.

So when Stacey, responsible for HR at Bodybuilding. com, explained the reason behind my lawyer's odd behaviour: avoiding calls, delayed replies and dodging questions, I hit the panic button. My visa, entitling me to live in the United States, had expired nearly a year earlier. My heart sank, because, while I didn't yet know the real implications, I knew this was serious. I had been working illegally and had overstayed my welcome in the country that I was calling home, by a significant margin.

In truth, the warning signs had been creeping up for some time. Bodybuilding.com had been chasing a tax number for their own records—one which would and should have been readily available from my lawyer if the latter hadn't been lying about the status of my visa. Inexplicably, it had never been extended when it ran out in 2009.

The obvious question, but one that is only truly obvious in hindsight, is how I could have let something so important slip under my nose. After all, it was my visa and ultimately, my responsibility. I know my strengths and I know my weaknesses—as any athlete must.

I am passionate about the things that I love. My work that revolves around helping people overcome the challenge of transformation is one of those things. It is all-consuming and success for me is spending each moment spreading the message of fitness and health to an ever wider audience. From my education in Sports Therapy in my early 20s in Wales through to my work at Bodybuilding.com where I could speak to millions, I have been passionate about my work.

Like a lot of people, paperwork is not my cup of tea. I'm not good at it and I know that. This is why employing somebody to help me jump over the many hurdles that are part and parcel of working in another country seemed like the right thing to do. And when a lawyer says everything is okay—you tend to presume that they know what they're talking about. Or at the very least, you presume they're being honest with you. A naïve thought.

Once the cold, hard panic had subsided, I turned to my friend Ryan Deluca for help. Like me and Stacey, he too was out of his depth as to what this meant and what could be the best course of action. We sat down with Bodybuilding.com's legal team and ran through the implications.

I am a positive person and despite the gravity of the situation, I believed wholeheartedly that because I hadn't done anything wrong, it would be resolved soon. I was raised on the solid principles that if you live your life with integrity, you will stay the course.

Amid the bad news and gloom that we had been left up a creek in Idaho without paddle by our lawyer, there was a silver lining of hope. We had uncovered the truth just four days before the one-year anniversary of my visa expiration. The year marker is an important one because the severity of punishment jumps: theoretically, from a three-five years ban from entering the USA again, to ten-fifteen years.

The lawyers were keen to keep me calm in this unprecedented chaos. They shared my optimism and instilled confidence in me that my lack of wrongdoing would save me from facing anything serious. But we decided that I would be helping my cause to leave the country and fight my corner on the altogether more solid ground of the United Kingdom.

Reassured, but still shaken, I began making surreal plans to exit the country within seventy-two hours.

I'm by no means a materialistic person but when I built a home in Boise I built it for life. The art that adorned the walls had been collected over the years. The garden had been nurtured and cared for from the time it was just a fledgling. A muddy patch had been sculpted into a tranquil Japanese-style oasis that provided solace from the hustle and bustle of daily life. I had poured my heart into every aspect of the interior design: from the glass-walled bathroom through to the bed I had shipped in. I had made a home out of a house. My home.

As I made frantic calls to find somebody to look after my pets, it occurred to me just how much I had to lose. I had built this world from scratch and only now that it was threatened did the true value of it dawn upon me.

Pushing this thought away, I shifted my focus to more important tasks at hand. I travelled to Las Vegas for the 46th Mr. Olympia competition. I tried to focus on the job of reporting the event for Bodybuilding.com and presenting the Bodybuilding.com supplement awards in front of thousands of enthusiasts. It is the character that dictates a person's reputation and despite my heartache, I knew I had to get the job done.

Nothing deters my focus. For instance, in the gym, I am able to isolate myself from the surrounding noise and make the work my focal point. When you shut out the distractions, you are in complete control of yourself and you can improve your optimum performance. Every athlete knows the feeling of being in that zone and most can attest to applying this same attitude to their lives. Control is power.

On that day however, I did not have control. My mind wandered and no matter what I did I could not stop thinking about Boise. And my future. There were too many question marks, conjectures and dilemmas.

Rather than sorting out who would take out my trash while I was away or what clothes to pack, I decided I would go to work.

The Mr. Olympia event, for those who have never attended, is the pinnacle of the bodybuilding year. I had grown up as a fan, in admiration of the athletes who showcased the extreme capabilities of the human body. I had been fortunate to cover the event as a reporter, brushing shoulders with idols. Later, I became close friends with many of them including Dorian Yates who dominated the competition scene during the '90s.

Apart from reporting the event for Bodybuilding.com's viewers, I was also presenting the supplement awards this year and amid the glitz, the glamour and the raw excitement, I felt dazed. The bad news and the sudden change in plan of action did not sit well in my carefully structured life. If you want to go fourteen years without missing a single meal, as I am proud to say I have, you need to plan and maintain certain structures that include: meal timing, meal prepping, carrying the meals in appropriate containers and cool bags depending on the duration of travel or being restricted within the vicinity of home and office, etc. When things go against these structures, I feel disconcerted. In my case, where I would be boarding a plane without the knowledge of my return, I wasn't enjoying the highlight of the bodybuilding calendar.

While I was keen to retain a sense of normality, I did have to leave Las Vegas early in order to make my way out of the States before my year deadline drew closer. Jay Cutler was going toe-to-toe with Phil Heath on his way to his fourth and, what was to be, his final title. But my mind was elsewhere now as I exited the competition scene and, having packed the bare minimum, made basic arrangements to be away for a few weeks.

Since I moved out of Wales for the first time in my early 20s, I had been back many times. I share a very close bond with my mother, father and sister and while I set out without looking back, I returned to the valleys of Wales when I could. This time, there was a sense that I had come full circle from my first journey.

When I made the decision to break away from the barriers of a lifestyle that was dragging me and my body down, I took control of my life. There was no big plan—I don't believe that there always has to be. Set yourself goals, make them long-term but don't expect to know where you want to be in fifteen years; the world is too interesting and complicated to know that from the beginning, especially if you've grown up in a small town in rural Wales.

My first transformation had taken place before I left and had propelled me to make that brave decision. With each of my consequential transformations, I took my body and my life into my own hands and moulded them into the shape that would allow me to grasp life by the horns. Each time, I had asserted further control over my destiny.

My life was in my hands. When I returned this time though, it was my head in my hands. Control over what happened next had passed to people I had little or no influence over. Even at that point, I didn't know the half of it.

Bodybuilding.com was a rock. The team could have patted me on the back and said "hard luck". They owed me nothing and there are plenty of budding writers who would have cut their arm off to take my place in the company. But Ryan and his legal team stood by me all the way and took on the battle of a lifetime.

My parents took up the fight with verve, too. And soon, we were compiling the evidence needed to help get me turn the clock back.

It did seem an altogether simpler matter when we began. The expectation was that I would be able to gather evidence that proved my innocence in the matter, the incompetence and dishonesty of our lawyer and ultimately that my residence and working in the country would only benefit the United States of America.

I made phone calls to people I hadn't heard from in years. I searched high and low for documentation I hadn't had to rely upon for decades. And all this while, I busted a gut to continue to do my day job remotely. It wasn't easy but after four weeks I was ready to face the music, and with a pile of paper as thick as my wrist, I made the journey to London to put my case forward to the US embassy.

Anyone who has been to an embassy will have shared the experience of faceless bureaucracy. As I took my seat holding the ticket and waited for my number to be announced, like a shopper waiting at the deli counter, I remained confident. When I left my home in the US, I was absolutely certain that I was moving in the right direction and that this would suffice.

The walls of any embassy reek of coldness and are soulless. They occupy corners of foreign countries representing their homeland with the character of a sidewalk. If you're lucky, you might spot a forlorn picture of a president or monarchy adorning the wall and a limp flag might hang behind the heads of bureaucrats stamping on forms with red ink. The country that you know is nowhere to be seen.

The US embassy in London, albeit grand, is no exception. The striking architecture looks more reminiscent of the Soviet Union than the economic powerhouse of the world. Were it not for an eagle perched on the roof, it would fade into the London skyline, as anonymous as the hundreds of other embassies flying solitary flags.

As I looked around the embassy, I couldn't see the United States that I loved. The Rockies didn't loom in the background. Nor did the hustle and bustle of New York City. The glamour I had left behind in Las Vegas with Mr. Olympia was but a distant memory. This was a world where passion and emotion didn't matter—rules did.

My number was called out and I strode as confidently as ever to the counter to put forth my case. But no sooner had I provided my name and details than I was told clearly that I had flouted the terms of my stay in the States.

The woman was emphatic, "When you overstay your welcome you forgo the opportunity to return. Thank you and good day. Next please."

I was gobsmacked. I pleaded with her that I knew I had overstayed my welcome but that if she would just look at my paperwork I was applying for a waiver to rectify this. The glazed over look told me that I was wasting my time.

"Next please."

In desperation, I began trying to explain the hundreds of pages of evidence in a handful of sentences, hopelessly tongue-tied.

"Next please. Sir, can you please move aside so that I can help the next customer."

Dejected, I stepped aside, perhaps realising that the third time of asking would probably invite the attention of the heavily-set men in black suits and sunglasses. I felt Boise, my pets, my home, my life, my career slipping through my fingers.

I have retained a lifelong stubborn streak of perseverance ever since the days I used to send countless articles to magazine editors, vying fruitlessly for their attention. Even when I don't know what I'm doing (or maybe especially when I don't), I remain adamant that I won't be beaten.

I phoned Ryan and the legal team to explain what had happened. Surely it was a mistake. Everything we had been told up until this point was that we had the evidence to fix this.

The situation had clearly gone out of hand and I was not prepared to imagine the worst. The legal team explained that when it comes to visas and letting you in and out of the country, the man or woman guarding the gate, in my case the haughty lady I had met at the embassy, has more power than the President of the United States. If they decide, perhaps on a whim or because they rolled out of bed on the wrong side, it doesn't matter what you do or say or have backing you: you're out of luck.

When I took that numbered ticket and approached the counter, I was doomed to fail. The woman was never going to say yes, no matter how nicely I smiled or how high I stacked my paper.

Exile is a word most commonly used to describe being sent away from your home. In my case, I had been exiled from the home that I had forged. It was like being jailed. I had no idea that whether I would be able to or could return. Dust gathered on my belongings in Idaho while I hit the drawing board once more.

With the support and advice from the team in the US, and my determination to not sit idle and let this happen to me, I began accumulating more paperwork. The clock was ticking and each stage, from pulling together evidence, through to applying for an appointment at the embassy to hearing back from them, was crucial.

All this time, weighing upon me was the burden of people I was letting down with my absence. Friends and colleagues aside, I had embarked on one of the biggest projects of my life, shortly before I left the US, in writing and publishing my first book: *Body by Design*. As part of the media promotion and launch, I should have been touring the States and shouting about it from the rooftops. Instead, I was stuck 5,000 miles away.

My options were running out and for the first time in my life, I was in despair.

My dad had other ideas though and was hunting high and low for another avenue. In time he enlisted the help of our local Member of Parliament, Roger Williams, who heard my plight and wrote a letter of support for me, to enable me to add weight to my argument.

Gradually, I collected further evidence of my worth in the industry I worked for, proof of my contribution to Bodybuilding. com, my book project with one of the world's largest publishers, right through to letters from other renowned publications and six times Mr. Olympia, Dorian Yates.

With my arsenal expanded, I returned to the bleak halls of the US embassy. I joined the queue, took my ticket and my seat once more. I was still confident. I still believed that I could bust my way out of exile thanks to the hard work and support of Bodybuilding.com and my family.

Mind drifting back to Boise, I was startled to hear someone call out my number. I leapt to my feet and approached the counter I had been called to from the ten windows available. Paper in hand, I prepared myself to explain my story from scratch.

Then, like a punch to the gut, I realised that standing behind the counter was the same woman who had sent me packing the first time. My heart sank but standing firm I observed that she didn't seem to have recognised me. I was just another unlucky sod who had been given the cold shoulder.

Raising the cover letter from the Minister of Parliament, I began to explain my overstay. But like an awful scene from Groundhog Day she clicked into mechanical action to tell me I had overstayed my visa and as a result forgone the right to return.

Flabbergasted I pleaded with her and requested her to read the letter, just to break from the script for a moment to entertain the idea that I might be worth more than a blank rejection.

"Next please." She exclaimed once more; this time, crushing me completely.

I broke down. For the first time since I had scared the living daylights out of myself on my motocross bike as a kid, brushing too closely to a disaster, I wept.

I was trapped in a nightmare without an escape. I had lost the control of the life I had spent fifteen years building. A life that was chronicled in the many pieces of paper I stood there clutching; paper that wasn't even worth a minute of this woman's time.

I was broken. But I was not beaten. I'll never be beaten.

2

Origins

The seeds of my perseverance were sown long before I learned the power of transformation and the despair of losing my life in the US. I was born in the heart of Wales in the UK in 1974. Wales is part of the United Kingdom, famed for its rugged landscape, aromatic tea and rugby. In the late 70s and the early 80s, when I was growing up, the country was going through tough times. The mining and agricultural industry—the backbone of the Welsh economy—was struggling and the once 'mighty' towns were boarding up shop windows and feeling the pinch of economic decline.

None of this mattered to me a great deal though. I was growing up on a farm with a loving family. The world was an adventure and in the rolling valleys, quarried hills and enchanted forests, I couldn't have been happier. It was a world away from the misery of redundancies and unemployment that many went through.

My parents were certainly more aware of the critical times but worked hard to make sure our family was okay. Working on a farm is a back-breaking career, though immensely rewarding. My mother and father were able to maintain a huge operation, whilst raising a family—no mean feat.

I often hear people decry the long hours they slog to hold down their job—how can they find time for the gym after the tiring hours at work? Working in a city is certainly stressful and tiring but on the farm, there's no let up. The work is physically and mentally challenging and can wear you out. Also, your graph of success is directly related to your efforts on the field. If you let something slip, you have to suffer the consequences all-year long. Responsibility lies with you and only you. You are accountable for every action you take, there's nobody to pick up the pieces when you fall.

Day starts long before most people have hit the snooze button and ends well after most are putting up their feet to watch television. And if, for example, a cow is in labour then long nights of blood, sweat and tears will follow. The work is your life. For the toil they endured for us, I'm eternally grateful to my parents.

The farm was big enough to allow more people to work there, and my parents managed the team very efficiently. The farm was always alive with different faces and characters that I could pester to play games and get up to some mischief or be adventurous.

Despite the farm buzzing with activities 24×7, I loved the solitude that this remote location offered me. The small town of Builth Wells was nearby and further afield several other market towns. But what dominated this part of our world were the looming hills, rolling valleys and the distant, often snow-capped, Brecon Beacons. This was a world where you could find solace, space and time to reflect in isolation. I have been an admirer of the serenity of this quaint little world since childhood, and my love has not diminished.

I was an explorer as a child. The farm was my playground and I was quick to adventure beyond its confines. Boundaries, either physical or drawn by my parents, were meant to be transgressed. I was always keen to travel beyond and explore the other side. I learned very early on that it was in this space—beyond where I was expected to be found—that I found myself.

By the time I could walk I was already trying to scale fences. And once I had done that I was in forests, hills and the nearby quarry. From the quarry, I could see Builth Wells and feel the energy of another world I might one day explore and be part of. Every horizon you reach creates your next and even at a young age I knew that I would always be driven by the want to reach another challenge, another destination.

In the forest I would walk for miles, setting snares across fences to capture rabbits and hunting for moles. In the yard I would erect ramps to ride over on my bike and everywhere I went I would look for an opportunity to push my adventures a step further.

There were times when my boldness would get the better of me. At the age of five, I stumbled upon a dead crow. It wasn't the first time I'd seen a dead animal, after all the passing of life is a recurring reality in a farm. But nestled amongst its black feathers was a bed of pulsing maggots. I'm still not quite certain why this bothered me so much but I remember the feeling of immediate revulsion clearly. I could not stand the parasites feasting upon the corpse of the bird.

I went to the shed where my father kept his petrol can for farm machines and other agricultural tools. I had learned from watching others that it could be used to incinerate dead animals so I decided to give some dignity to the dead. I returned with the can and some matches I managed to find on the lower shelf.

I dowsed the crow in petrol, hopelessly unsure about the quantity thinking it was better to have too much than too little. The match carefully lit as I shuffled towards the crow and threw the light onto it. Unfortunately, I had drastically overestimated the amount of petrol needed and the flames jumped up scorching my eyebrows.

The experience left me shaken. But as my mother wiped the singed hair from my face, I couldn't help but feel proud that I'd done the job myself. There was another episode when I had wanted to unplug the television without asking for help. Older plugs had a tendency to stick, so when I was unable to yank it from the wall I decided to use my father's tin tobacco box to lever it away. Again, I felt smug about my inventiveness. But as I wedged it in, lent backwards and levered it out from the wall I was thrown off the ground, landing five feet away. I learned the hard way about the dangers of fire and electricity!

Such misadventures have led my thrill for individual pursuit, first in motocross and then in the gym. I've always preferred tackling things on my own. The sense of responsibility, lying solely on my shoulders, drives me forward. When I win, I alone enjoy the thrill. When I lose, I bear the brunt of shame and disappointment. I am accountable to my harshest critic.

The collision course with motocross was inevitable. Mid-Wales has long been home to motorsports thanks to its varied landscape and the weather that poses a challenge to even the most experienced drivers and riders. My father enjoyed riding too and it wasn't long, at the age of six, before I was clambering aboard knackered, old rusty wheels and feeling the rush of excitement as an engine roared beneath me.

I was never a natural and my small frame never lent well to the shape of the bikes. One thing I had on my side though was raw passion for pushing bikes to the limit. I thrived on the very fear that pushed many bikers back. It didn't stem from an ill-founded sense of invulnerability. I knew well from watching just how serious accidents on bikes could be. On the contrary,

I loved the fear. I loved pushing myself well beyond my own ability and letting the bike take control.

Interest in the sport soon flourished into a passion and after I started to get reasonably skilled in my early teens, I was picked up by a local garage for some low level sponsorship. With one of the newly-imported Suzukis on my side, I could really hit the ground running.

Words will fail me if I attempt to describe this sport. Even a video cannot capture the adrenaline surge adequately. I would often arrive at the course, all across the UK, and nervously inspect the track. I'd have every corner and every bend internalised, so that I could fly through the course without waiting to see what awaited me beyond the next hill or twist.

At its core, the sport is about taking a lightweight motorcycle as fast as possible around a mud track filled with every twist, turn, jump or obstacle imaginable. The rider, with helmet and guards to shins, knees, shoulders and elbows, hangs on as the bike tears up the ground. The roar of the twin-stroke (or four-stroke, now) engine ripples as the bike nips across the ground and even at a standstill it seems to bubble with excitement raring to go.

The entire experience gets your blood pumping. But when you fling yourself into a corner with six other riders, wheels spinning, engines peaking, all trying desperately to find solid ground to thrust themselves forward again—the adrenaline is at full flow. As you approach the jump you don't even get the time to let the fear take hold. The ground disappears and for a split second you're as weightless as an astronaut hurtling through space and then, just as quickly, back towards earth with a crunch. Briefly, you can take a gulp of air, as you attempt to regain balance and prepare to weave through the next line of obstacles.

I suffered from asthma during my growing up years and I remember I had to be rushed to the hospital on one occasion. But this didn't prevent me from approaching the track with undying confidence and belief. That confidence was, however, beset by uncontrollable nerves. Whenever we pulled into the car park for a race, I would invariably feel sick to my core. While I believed in my own ability I couldn't brush aside this mixture of nerves and excitement.

On the starting line, my focus would be absolute and mind wouldn't falter. When the light flashed green, I had already driven the first three corners in my mind. While I was busy looking over the horizon, the bike took over. I was never one to let my ability determine the bike's speed. I knew that as long as I gave the engine full throttle I could hang on for dear life.

This tactic served me well to a point and I was competing on the national circuit at quite a young age.

This would be the first of many runner-up spots in my career. I was able to achieve such a rank because I was adept in bad weather. When most people would slow down in the rain, as mud splattered over spectators and competitors alike, I would speed up. I loved the fizz of bike beneath me when the weather closed in, water pouring down the visor and making it all the more difficult to see. I lived for the moment when I had thrown myself too fast off a jump and come crashing down with just enough balance to continue. The fear of riding beyond my skill level was addictive: dangerously so.

My first crash wasn't an overly serious one. It happened on the first event of a four-leg day in Rhayader, when I was seven. As always, I had the pedal to the floor going through the course as though I was on fire. The next moments are fragmented but I must have hit a bump at the wrong angle because my front wheel locked up and I had the sensation I was watching myself from above. I was bruised and shaken but I was able to walk away. I had pushed myself too far, allowed the bike to take too much control. I didn't race again that weekend, but the next Saturday, I was roaring down the track once more in search of the adrenaline.

There were many more crashes over the years, often serious, but I learned to cope. An adrenaline junky knows that there are dangers, they are part of the trade off you make in order to pursue your passion. While I enjoyed practising on my own it was only when I hit the track with competition that I could enjoy the fruits of my work.

One of my next door neighbours was a guy called Paul Rowlands. He was one of the people who encouraged me to race and he went on to become a British champion for two wheel enduro. He was also one of the first people to get into the new sport of quad-biking, small motorbike-like vehicles with four wheels that are great for off-roading.

A few years ago, whilst racing one of these on a beach in the South-West of England, the water spray became so great that he was unable to see a slowing vehicle in front of him. Paul collided with it, coming off his quad. The racers behind him couldn't see either and came clattering into his helpless body. His suffered life-threatening injuries and when he woke up to find himself paralysed from the waist down, he was happy to have survived.

I do remember being devastated by the news but when I went to see him he was in good spirits. He always knew the odds of something like that happening and he went from strength to strength in the following years despite being unable to walk.

Although I have never mentioned this to him, he has been my inspiration with his attitude and work ethic ever since that fateful day. He never let the accident hold him back. He hoped to recover but that wasn't his focal point. Instead, he established a large and successful Welsh development company and now runs an equally successful motocross team. Paul is a perfect example of someone who looks at a glass half full and knows how to control his environment rather than letting it control his ambitions.

He even had a quad modified in order that he could ride it again. The sport was his passion and he could never regret pursuing it.

It is the same driving emotion in any sport. You can enjoy going to the gym on your own, you can enjoy running on your own, you can enjoy racing on your own. But to love a sport, you need to find others and share the joy with them. In a competition, your efforts are put into perspective and you get an opportunity to relate or compare your achievement vis-à-vis others. It's the one place where you are all truly accountable for your efforts.

As a personal trainer and transformation specialist, I come across many people who want to improve their fitness and health for their own enjoyment and benefit. This is a good attitude to have toward fitness and health. But I still encourage these people to consider competition at the end of their transformations. First and foremost, it gives them a goal to work towards and a sense of achievement when they have completed it, however or whichever way they do it. Moreover, it cultivates accountability and a sense of responsibility. When you know you're going to be judged for your efforts, it spurs you on to go further and faster.

So, while my passion was the riding itself, it was only in competition that I experienced that rush. And each time I earned success I started thinking about the next competition. As in bodybuilding and fitness, you should never allow your goals to arrive and pass. That is when you lose your motivation and purpose. At every horizon, don't stop thinking about what lies beyond. Enjoy reaching your goals but enjoy the journey even more.

By the time I was in my mid-teens, I was competing most weekends from February through to November, accumulating points as part of a season. In my mind, I excelled at it, because I loved doing it.

I was never destined to enjoy school, from the first day when I got there. I remember vividly that the first day of school was a day that I had planned to spend in the forest, but I was coaxed away from my adventures by my mother who said we were going to the local primary school to have a chat with a teacher. Reluctant but unaware of what this meant I decided to postpone my venture for another day. When we arrived at the grey walls of Llanelwedd Primary, I was sent to play in the sandpit, where I set about digging holes and building castles.

When I stopped for a moment in my work, I looked up to find, alarmingly, that my mother had disappeared. I interrogated the woman she had been talking to and was told that she had gone over the bridge to town for the day and would be back in a bit. I had been hoodwinked.

In my five-year-old mind, it was a traumatic event. And while I was wrong to be worried, I was right to be sceptical. School and I did not get along. It wasn't that I didn't like to learn, I just didn't find any interest in what I was being taught. Mathematics dealt with numbers that meant nothing to me. Science was the study of forces I couldn't see and chemicals I'd never heard of. It all felt so irrelevant to a boy who wanted to explore the real and tangible world.

I did enjoy things I could do with my hands, making things in metalwork or learning how to cook. Sadly, these subjects were looked down upon (they are still today, to some extent) as less academic and considered less worthwhile. If they had been more than fillers, I might have ended up on an entirely different path.

Music was the one lesson I enjoyed week in week out, partly because we were allowed to slip away into practice rooms where we could eat biscuits, and mostly because it was another of my passions that I'd always wanted to nurture. At home, my parents introduced me to rock music at a very early age. I was well versed in Led Zeppelin, Cream and Deep Purple by the time most of my friends were still crooning nursery rhymes.

By the time I was six I was listening to Billy Idol and I adored and respected music as a form of expression. It created a world into which I subsumed myself. Sadly, the music we were taught at school felt an entire world away from the vibrant, edgy and energetic pulse that was emerging in the early punk-rock era. In fact, it's probably fair to say that my only teenage aspiration was to be in a band, though I never quite developed the guitar skills to do so.

Instead, I focused my attentions on the dirt track. As I grew older I could take on bigger bikes and scarier tracks. I could raise the fear level as I desired and although I could never lay claim to being brilliant, my stubborn perseverance and love of pushing the boundary of my skill and daring meant that I was successful.

I continued to ride through my teens and into my 20s. With the support of the local garage, I had a bike to match my ambition and I spent a great deal of time learning how it worked and how it could be improved—adding carbon fibre manifolds, modifying the pedals to provide better grip and generally tweaking—to gain those extra seconds that made all the difference.

At some point, I started to lose my love for the sport though. Perhaps it was also tied to my growing weariness with my career path. I had left school at 16 and decided to take on an engineering course to develop my mechanical skills and potentially get some maintenance work at a local factory. The scope for creativity was nil, I felt as constrained, controlled and constricted as I had at school. Nothing about it excited me and I didn't know or enjoy where it was going.

I left the course and got work lacquering wood at a local factory; the work was okay but the people were great. It was a step up if not into something I loved. I was enjoying becoming an adult and going out to drink with friends. But I was on an inevitable path to nowhere and my body was losing its shape as I found I could no longer eat and drink what I wanted.

At the same time I was feeling the pain of more than fifteen years of motocross. I had developed a bad back from an accident where the front tyre of my bike had gotten stuck in the ground and I had torn muscles in my right trap and lats. It was excruciating but the painful memories had eventually faded. Although I could feel my whole body begin to deteriorate, what I didn't realise at the time was that my riding style on the bike was giving me a curved spine, putting pressure on my back and causing discomfort in my day to day life. It was a slow and depressing experience that didn't happen overnight or in a single accident. Slowly, my physique suffered and I started losing interest in the sport.

As I went through countless, different medical procedures with absolutely no relief, I realised that both motocross and an unhealthy lifestyle had taken a toll on my body. After trying just about every remedy that was offered by professionals, I turned to a friend called Anthony Bridgeman whose suggestion helped me deal with the medical hurdles. Anthony was a weight-trainer and taught me useful exercises that I could try to rehabilitate my muscles.

The results were astonishing. Over a matter of weeks I felt relief from a condition that had been severely affecting me for months. The experience compelled me to think about my body and how I was looking after it. If such a small amount of weight training could have such a drastic effect, what would happen if I were to really set my mind to it?

Another friend, Mark Davies, was a bodybuilder and invited me to come along to hit the weights. The aim was to transform my physique. This was a whole different level.

Some people find the gym an intimidating place to begin with. When you first step inside, from the busy outside world, and you're faced with a clinical environment filled with people straining their bodies, it feels like an alien place. It's one of the most common excuses you hear from many people trying to get into shape at home rather than a gym where they might have access to better equipment.

When you find yourself at that stage of life where you've decided you need to make a change, the sight of people looking better should not make a difference or demotivate you in any way. You should be determined to achieve your goal. The truth is most people at the gym might be conscious of being in a public space but that doesn't discourage them from entering their own zone, the zone that allows them to be free of the distraction around. Their focus is only on themselves.

There was a twinge of embarrassment when I first arrived, but I was confident of the little rehab work I'd undertaken earlier and I knew within that I might enjoy it. The hit was almost instantaneous. I took my first set of reps and pushed hard. As I finished I felt a rush that I'd only had on the motocross tracks before. I wanted more and more.

The back pain was soon a distant memory and I was going from strength to strength. I loved having control over my body and as soon as I had my headphones on and began pumping my muscles, I could immediately feel the work pressure and anxiety being wiped away.

My motocross career was coming to a natural end. Not because I wasn't doing well. In fact, I had been told I could get a sponsorship from E.T. James' Suzuki Motorcycles if I moved into enduro racing—where I could race around the track for a full day. The trouble was that enduro racing lacked the very element I loved about motocross—hurling myself around as quickly as possible. It simply became a drag to try and keep a moderate pace for a full day. There was no passion and certainly no sense of living on the edge of my ability. I needed a new challenge.

I had flickered between jobs and while I didn't dislike the work I was doing I didn't know where it was going. I had always been ambitious on the track and I felt as though I needed to start applying that to my life as well. Working as a ground labourer on scaffolding had taught me how miserable it could be in the cold, wet and windy Wales. I didn't last long there. I was partying all the while and though I was feeling better from my work in the gym I began to sense that bodybuilding could mean more than just a hobby.

I was training at the local college gym during that time. I enjoyed going there because it was full of people my age and there were plenty of budding bodybuilders from whom I could learn more. One of the teachers at the college happened to be Daryl Aldis. Daryl was a very successful bodybuilder and had won Mr. Britain despite a 5'5" frame. He had a wealth of knowledge that I yearned to tap into and eventually I plucked up the courage to approach him and seek advice on training from him.

As a rookie your instinct always makes you presume that the big shots won't have time for you. On the contrary, the truth is most are happy to impart some knowledge. Everyone started somewhere and fitness is an evangelical pursuit: once you know the truth you're desperate to share it. Never be afraid to look up to the people, who have spent a lifetime learning how the body works, for advice—they'll have plenty of suggestions and advice on the things you should avoid and stay away from.

Daryl was kind to spare his time and, in return for some chicken breasts from my parents' farm, he offered me training and nutritional advice. Much of this advice wouldn't be found in books and was invaluable in helping me understand some of the elementary concepts of health, fitness and nutrition that I diligently follow, for both my transformation work and my own diet, even today.

For all we have learned about the world, from the highest mountains, to the dense rainforests and even into the stars, we know startlingly little about the one thing that we all have: our bodies. Our diets and our activities have completely altered in the last hundred years but despite that, there is very little that we have done to accommodate a healthy style of living. We are willing to rely on the plethora of 'fat free' and 'sugar free' options but little do we care about how to nourish our trillion cells within our body with the right food for a healthy living. Our priorities need to change as far as our diet is concerned; we are yet to educate ourselves and understand how to maintain lifestyles that don't destroy our bodies.

Understanding is vital. That's why, only the knowledge of beneficial exercises and strict diet rules was insufficient for me to get into shape. I wanted to know why. I wanted to understand the dynamics in greater depth so that I could improve and expand, to go further and faster. Just like when my father tweaked and added parts to my motocross bike, I wanted to know my body inside out so that I could modify and better it—initially to heal my injuries, and eventually to realise its real potential.

I knew that my exchanging of chicken breasts for advice could only get me so far. So I returned to the one place I had had little to no success thus far in life, school, or rather college. During one of my increasingly frequent trips to the college gym, I enquired the availability of places on a course. I discovered, to my amazement, that not only there were spaces but a grant was available too.

I applied without much contemplation. Although I had been exposed to this world for only a handful of months I knew there was something meaningful in this. My parents were supportive, like they have always been, and stood behind my change of direction without any questions. I stopped motocross, now long a burden rather than a love, and reduced my work to part-time to support my education.

Back to school again I found what I had been missing. Everything we studied wasn't just relevant, it was revolutionary. The course was Sports Therapy and the college was nationally renowned for the quality of study and the faculty. Now, Daryl was one of my teachers and I was learning from other experts who explained theories behind hunches I had begun to develop from figuring out how the body worked.

This education isn't to be underestimated and I always emphasise on its importance when I provide personal training. Such is the pace at which you learn about the body in terms of the exercises and the nutrition it demands. It is when you begin understanding the basics you realise just how little you have scratched the surface of potential that is there. In my case, a flame had been lit and my thirst for knowledge quenched because of the course I was studying.

I certainly hadn't stopped partying though and I continued to precariously balance these two disparate segments of my life. On the one hand I would drink until the early hours with a group of friends, making a fool of myself, but enjoying nonetheless; I was excelling at my studies and spending increasing amounts of time in the gym on the other. I was beginning to take charge of my life with a firm grip. But it would take my first transformation to truly realise what the future has in store for me.

3

A Journey Begins

I'd seen them from afar, on the glossy pages of magazines. These superhumans. They fascinated me but they seemed so distant. These sculpted bodies were beyond the limits of my imagination. It was another world.

I had been hitting the gym for around eighteen months, and that world was still a million miles away from me. I was working hard on my course and, each day, I knew I was getting closer to something I really believed in. It was invigorating. But still, I had these two paths running parallel to one another. Two different lives that co-existed side by side but could never fit together. My new-found challenge? Or the easy comfort of a drink with friends?

I could have gone either way, to be honest, had it not been for the day that showed me exactly where I wanted to go. Since those early days when I'd gotten tips from Daryl Aldis, through three years of teaching, I'd grown increasingly interested in his technique of bodybuilding.

At the end of my diploma, I decided to go along with him to one of the events he was competing at. I wasn't sure what to expect but I was curious. As is often the case, that curiosity led me down the rabbit hole and much further.

The event wasn't a big one—the Mansfield Classic—but it was enough to blow me away. I had seen bodybuilders before. I had seen the world's greatest, plastered across magazine covers and on television shows. This was the first time I was seeing them in the flesh.

It was like watching a 3D film for the very first time. As they took to the stage, pumped and tanned, their bodies had a physicality that is impossible to recreate. I had entered the world of the superhumans. It felt as though I had jumped inside my comic books and I was standing amongst my own superheroes. Except, this was very real.

On the drive back my mind was racing. That universe, backdropped by the Venice beach in Los Angeles had seemed so completely unattainable at the start of the day. But at the Mansfield, I had been within touching distance of a fraction of that world.

Things finally started to crystallise in my mind. As wonderful as my childhood had been, as much as I loved my family and as fond as I was of Wales, I needed to escape. I wasn't sure where I needed to be but that window into the world of bodybuilding showed me it wasn't Builth Wells. And as exciting as Daryl's competition had been, I sensed that as long as I was in Wales I would be tempted by my other life. I needed a clean break.

I was twenty-four and up until this point things had moved quite slowly. I had flickered between all manner of jobs, locally, and my motocross had stuttered to a halt whilst I gradually picked up weight training and got engrossed in my diploma work. Three years had passed since I found my passion but I was still in two minds as to where it was leading me. After that day, things began to accelerate. And quickly.

As soon as I got home I grabbed my copy of *Muscle News* magazine and furiously scanned the calendar. I knew exactly what I had to do in order to change my life—I needed to go through a transformation. But I also yearned for a goal to get me there. Something that would be impossible for me to ignore, something so terrifyingly out of my depth that I wouldn't dare turn back. That something was a competition.

It was early autumn, so I knew my options were limited. The season finished in November and there was a long winter of temptations to get through before the next cycle started in March. Anyway, that meant a very long wait—I needed instant inspiration. I had to act upon this impulse to change my life.

There it was, Pontypridd in November. It was tight—in fact it gave me only eight weeks to get ready—but I knew it had to be done. I set the date and worked out how I would get there. No excuses.

In the meantime, I was still thinking about my next course of action. With the possibility of a future elsewhere, an opportunity was swift to follow. A few weeks after Daryl's competition, the college held an event where they invited various companies' heads to come and talk to us about placement opportunities and how we could put our diplomas to use.

For all my anticipation, I was left disappointed by most of the avenues. The jobs were fine but they didn't really promise the jump-start I wanted to broaden my experience and whet my appetite for the world of bodybuilding.

Finally, a company called Steiner came to talk to us about cruise ships. The sell was an easy one. Its staff travelled from destination to destination providing beauty and fitness treatment to clients along the way. You could also explore and enjoy everything from the Caribbean to the Mediterranean while on the job. And if you worked hard, you would be rewarded as well. To a twenty four-year-old looking to escape, it seemed like a no-brainer. Here was a company that would pay me to travel the world, practise my trade and have a good time. My only thought was "Where do I sign up?"

Without hesitation I did exactly that, putting in an application. Within a few weeks I was called for an interview in Swansea for the role, which went smoothly. The only drawback was that I would have to remove the piercings I had got done over the years. But I figured this was a small price to pay for a ticket around the world. I would have to wait some time for an answer. Meanwhile, I went back to focussing on the more pressing matter of my physical transformation for the competition in Pontypridd.

This was the first time I'd ever done anything like this and I was finding my way in the dark a little tough to tread. What I had learned over nearly three years during my course gave me some clues, and help from Daryl and others at the gym uplifted my confidence, but competitive bodybuilding was something entirely different.

Normally, an athlete would give themselves up to twenty weeks, or at least twelve to get in shape. I had less than two months, so the pressure was on. I wasn't in terrible shape but I had plenty of body fat to lose and very little time to do so. I couldn't afford to slowly bulk myself up and trim the fat. I needed to go lean, and fast.

I began my brutal routine at 5 a.m. every day, with an hour of cardio. Post that, I attended college followed by work at the lacquer factory. After work, I'd do weights and another hour of cardio. Depending on the day of the week, I could then have a shift at a bar I was working at. By any measure, I couldn't afford to waste time. And even if I could I didn't want to because I knew that if I stopped, even for an hour, I might have time to dwell on the possibility of not reaching my goal or I might allow the cravings for food and alcohol to breed.

The hardest thing of all was cutting out the carbs. For lack of a better idea, I did it completely. No carbohydrates to fuel my long days. I was certain that my body would run entirely off the body fat I needed to lose. The idea seemed to work to begin with and my weight and body fat plummeted. Then, of course, as my body fat reached near nought I slowly started to pay the price, shedding some of my muscles and of course, my sanity.

After nearly six weeks in, the hallucinations started. I would go to get money from a cash machine and suddenly find myself in a conversation with it. I'd do things like putting coffee away in the fridge. Driving home from work became a tangle. I had eked out every drop of energy from my day's food and I was incapable of navigating the dark country roads. Inevitably, I would take every wrong turn possible. It was like being stuck in a recurring nightmare.

Of course, in hindsight, I didn't need to go to these lengths. In fact, with the muscle loss it even began to prove counterproductive. But I was finding my way, testing my body to see what worked and what didn't. Most of all I was determined that I would turn up in Pontypridd in phenomenal shape, whatever the cost.

My weight was dropping quickly, eventually reaching sixty-nine kilos. I knew I was going to be the smallest competitor there so I had to be the leanest. My separation from and definition of each muscle group would need to be my ally. Then of course, there was the tanning and the posing. I began practising these, either at home or at work when everyone else had left. I had only what I'd picked up from Daryl to go on, so this was probably the area I felt most unsure about.

As the day approached the nerves kicked in. Being on stage in front of an audience and judges was the final test for all of my work. The past couple of years since I had first stepped into a gym had been building up to this and the past eight weeks provided the penultimate boost. With time as a limited resource, I was managing a crisis situation.

Many people noticed the dramatic transition in my body and its shape, but only one person knew what I was planning to achieve by the end of it. I had told Mark Davies, not because I needed somebody to be accountable to (I am my biggest critic) but because I wanted somebody to share the moment with me. And Mark had been the friend who had first encouraged me to take my rehabilitation work further and into bodybuilding.

Pontypridd had been such an obvious choice because it was relatively close by, just an hour from where I lived. The event was well set for me and I was joining other first timers. By the time the day arrived I was undoubtedly reaching the very end of my physical transformation and I really don't know how much longer my body or brain could have withstood the regime I had it under.

We made the short drive and arrived well before the registration desk even opened. Waiting impatiently I got myself a coffee from the nearby petrol station, feeling the fatigue of eight weeks of hard work. When the desk opened an hour later, I was first in line and learned that I would be on stage an hour and a half later. Now I could really begin psyching myself up.

Back in the car I raised my legs onto the dashboard and put the heating on full. I was determined to sweat every ounce of water weight out of me. Then I went backstage and began to pump up with the weights available to fill the muscles with blood and the carbohydrates I fed them the day before. Slowly but surely I could feel myself transforming and by the time I had my tan on, you would barely have recognised me from the person who had gone to Daryl's competition eight weeks before.

This was an all-Wales competition, so it was no soft opener. Amongst the judges and the photographers were stalwarts from the bodybuilding world. The pressure was mounting and as I stood backstage with the other competitors I realised I was out of luck. Despite all my hard work, these guys seemed huge, colossal, hulks of men. I took solace in the pride that I'd made it this far.

My apprehension was premature, though. The beauty of bodybuilding is that until you're on stage facing your competitors, you can't really tell who's got it and who doesn't. The goliath back stage can wilt under the spotlight. The bodybuilder, who appears the largest, when backstage, can look the smallest when the fake tan is difficult to hide under the bright lights on stage. The tan and lights could either help highlight every fat-free muscle making the bodybuilder look larger than life, or else can give away the true story of an unprepared contestant. A softer muscle that has a layer of fat on will look a lot worse under the piercing light.

As I climbed onto the stage and took part in the symmetry round, followed by the muscularity round and finally the posing round, I began to realise that I was doing myself proud. Sure, I thought, I'm not here to win but this is the proof I needed. I had transformed my body and I was in the best shape of my life by a country mile. I was ready to take on the world now. As the judges deliberated which six competitors would make to the final round from the dozens of pretenders there, I sat down in the corner and took a deep breath.

To this day, I've never been wholly comfortable in front of crowds and cameras. I don't get the same buzz from performing for others that I do for myself. So when I got off the stage, the overwhelming emotion had subsided and I felt a big relief. I began to reflect upon the last eight weeks and how they had changed me. Not just physically but mentally.

No sooner had I relaxed my nervous system than I got the shock of a lifetime. My name was among the six finalists. This caught me off guard.

Before I knew, I was back on stage, posing once more with the other competitors. This was surreal. The camera flashed and dazed me while my mind drifted. I focused once more and made eye contact with the judges, trying to show the confidence that I knew I had but was momentarily cloaked by my nerves.

Again, I clambered off the stage and awaited the news, this time with a little more than passing interest. The names were read out in reverse order.

"Fifth place..." *Queue*: polite applause.

"Fourth place..." More applause.

"Third place..." Louder applause, again.

"Second place, Kris Gethin." I felt a swell of pride that I hadn't quite expected.

"And first place..." Cheers welcomed the guy standing next to me and his victory as he punched the air.

Quietly, I slipped away with a grin on my face. Sceptics would probably doubt my jubilance and question why I wasn't bitter at finishing second. The truth is it had never been about the finishing line for me, it was entirely about the journey I had been on to get there. I had to enter the race in order to have touched that finish line, without worrying what position I crossed the line in. To have been declared the 'second' best was nothing but a bonus.

I had pummelled my body in the last eight weeks to an extent that I would never recommend anyone else doing. I had to do it though and I had found out more about myself and my body during that crucial period than in the previous twenty-four years. Physically and mentally I was a different person and the only thing that could stop me now was the inevitable comedown from such a build up.

Exhausted, I made my way home. As we pulled into the driveway at my parents' house, I saw my father leaving for somewhere. Up until this point only Mark knew where we had been during the day and while I wasn't desperate to hide what I'd been up to, I couldn't be sure how people would react. After all, going to the gym is one thing but donning fake tan and posing on stage isn't exactly commonplace in rural Wales.

I did think for a moment I might get away with it but I could tell from my father's face that I'd forgotten something. "What's the tan about?" he asked. I wanted to lie but I couldn't so I explained that I'd been at a bodybuilding competition. "Well, how did you get on?" he prompted me, to my surprise. I told him that I'd been awarded the second position, smiling now that the cat was out of the bag. "Well done then," he replied and said he was on his way. My father is a straightforward character, that's something I've always appreciated. The same goes for both my parents, they have supported me through the crests and the troughs along the way, never questioning my choices—only wishing me well and offering sound advice.

The respite was short, which was a good thing, because it didn't allow my momentum to deflate. A few days later I received a letter from Steiner asking me to join them for training. I'd nailed the interview and now I was heading to London. That's when it started to feel real. I'd been planning to leave Wales for some time but this was the confirmation that I was ready. I had completed my first transformation, taken most of the competition by storm and now I was on course for a new life.

When I look back on that first transformation, I can see how important it was to my overall development as a person.

It was the first time I took life under my control and showed my potential. All that time spent in school where every report card I'd ever got had said, "Easily distracted" and "Must try harder" had been turned on its head in those three years of my diploma in Sports Therapy. And when I took on those eight weeks capped by the competition, I was conforming to the rules and levels of dedication that I had abided by—though in patches—during my motocross career.

I was just following my nose. I had found something that interested me and I wanted nothing more than to pursue it as far as I could. I had acted on impulse when I entered the competition and not allowing myself a spare second to consider giving up had pulled me through. Steiner had given me the perfect pitch for the mindset I was in.

I think, that's how it has been for me; I follow my instinct and while I make plans and goals, I tend to situate myself into the unknown without the knowledge where it's going to lead eventually me.

With just those couple of weeks to prepare, I departed Wales with the wind in my sail. I was unsure for how long, but I was confident that I was going in the right direction—which is about all I could hope to know.

4

Sailing to Freedom

My experience with Steiner could be best summed up in a single word: escape. I knew I needed to get away from Wales and I wanted to do something that was vaguely fitness related. This fitted the description and looked like a whole lot of fun.

Travelling down to London from Wales, I was looking forward to the new opportunity, but nothing had been set in stone. The next step was training, which in effect was another kind of an interview.

I clenched my faintly-bruised fist as the fields flew past the train window and I gritted my teeth. I had left Builth Wells in a flurry of emotions. A relationship with a girl had broken down and anger and hurt lingered. I needed to escape and it had to be soon.

I had been a shy kid and most of the girls I knew didn't interest me much. As a college student, people I came across didn't have the same approach to fitness I had; they were either on beauty training courses or else looking to lose a few pounds before going back to normal life.

Suzie was different. She hailed from the Lake District and spoke with a soft northern accent. Her bright eyes and a wild streak appealed to my slightly oddball self. She wasn't ordinary and that's what I really liked about her. She was the only girl who was genuinely interested in bodybuilding. I couldn't believe my luck meeting someone like her in Mid Wales: she was one of a kind.

That was my first proper relationship. Her electric personality was a joy to be around, although we did struggle through a few tumultuous phases where her fiery nature played against us. Toward the end of my college course, I had begun to work on my transformation and I started to sense that something wasn't right. Unfortunately, my fears didn't prove to be groundless.

A few days before the competition, I found out that Suzie had been sleeping with one of my friends. My heart sank. I was crushed to learn the harsh truth and didn't know how to come to terms with the bitter revelation. Blood drained from my face as I realised the power of a handful of words.

As part of my fitness regime, I had been living a carbohydrate-free life for weeks and what little energy I did have was being soaked up by my full days of work and training. My body throbbed with anguish. No sooner had my heart sunk than a wave of hurt arose through me and filled my chest as I desperately began searching for meaning in this chaos I had found myself in.

With my head spinning, I raced around to the house where the friend who Suzie had been with was living. I had no idea what I was going to say; I hadn't prepared myself for something like this. I had been conquered by an overwhelming urge to let him know that I knew. I wasn't going to hit him, but I had to confront him. Confrontation was something I hated but I had to go against my dislike this time.

I pulled up nearby. The guy was the drummer in a band, several of whom were friends of mine. I had calculated, with the little sense I had in me that he would be on his own now.

As I got out of my car though, two other friends from the band pulled up, greeted me and began walking with me to the door.

It was the clincher, I couldn't have turned back—I would have to see him.

As he opened the door, I kept my eyes fixed to the ground. I couldn't look at him. I couldn't bring myself to establish eye contact. The pent-up hurt in my chest yearned to spill over. I could feel it turning hot and white. I remember my fingers curling into a fist and clenching, so as to hold back my anguish. He said hello to the other guys first and then greeted me.

The next thing I know he's lying on the ground. That hot and white flash had accumulated in my fist and I reacted at the sound of his voice. A voice that thought I didn't know what he had been doing. I don't remember the moment but I had hit him square on the jaw. It wasn't revenge, just pain and reflex.

The two other friends now held my arms and were trying hard to tear me back—my new-found physique surging toward him. He half-picked himself up, wiping the few drops of blood from his jaw and nursing his face. As he scrambled away, not looking back to meet my eyes, I began to take control of myself again.

I explained my actions to the friends who had just witnessed this outburst. They listened and nodded, clearly taken aback that I had gone from being a zero to full tilt in such a short span of time.

The bodybuilding competition in Pontypridd was still days away but that was a defining moment, a turning point, when I arrived at a decision. I needed to get out of there. The experience had wrecked my faith in relationships and left me feeling certain that Builth Wells was not my future. There had to be something bigger and better. Anything had to be better than what I was going through.

The training for Steiner took place in the outskirts of London in a place called Stanmore. If you're picturing the London of the films, with the glamour of the West End, the imperial architecture with history looming above and the booming city bankers, think again. Stanmore is classic London suburbia where the drab 1970s houses merge with dull business parks. The saving grace was being on the tube line from where I could regale in the beauty of the parks and green patches few and far between central London. It was a breath of fresh air after the last few weeks.

The training course was an aptitude test of sorts where candidates from all over the world came to learn their trade. Stanmore was Steiner's international training centre, so while I might have been underwhelmed by the surroundings, I suspect those travelling from the States and elsewhere must have been left even more disappointed. Over the few weeks we were together, the idea was that our performance would dictate where and when we joined a cruise. It was competition time, again.

I was staying in the local YMCA with the other candidates. It was a liberating experience meeting such a diverse group of people from various backgrounds and corners of the earth. I was sharing a room with a stereotypically slick Italian and a quiet Czech but there were men and women from South Africa, America, Canada...the list goes on.

One of the people I met was a Canadian called Jason St. Marie. He was a fantastic guy with an incredible sense of humour and a sharp dress sense. I didn't know it then, but years later we would again meet back stage at The World Natural Bodybuilding Championship in Canada, both competing in different weight classes. During the training period, he was one of the few candidates who shared my growing interest in bodybuilding and we stuck together through the three weeks.

The training itself was relatively straightforward and I took to it without any discomfort. My course in Wales had been so comprehensive that I could handle almost anything they threw at me.

In fact, the only thing I needed to brush up on was facials which did catch me slightly off guard and out of my comfort zone. As I awkwardly fumbled through the programme, I learned the hard way that if you go against the grain on a man's stubble with a cotton bud he ends up looking like Santa Claus. Slowly, but surely, I started picking up the basics; while that wasn't exactly an engaging exercise compared to the other elements of the programme, I was happy to give it a go.

It wasn't all training and we could find time in the evening to go out drinking. I soon discovered what an international sport drinking could be. And since I hadn't yet shaken off my partying habits from Wales, with a new crowd here, I was eager to have a good time and let myself loose. Often, a little too loose.

One such night I went out with Jason and before we knew it a couple of pints became a skinful. I was out of control and more than I even realised. When I woke up the next day with a hell of a hangover, I was surprised to see my Czech room-mate staring angrily at me from across the room. We'd gotten along fine up until then, so I wondered what I could have done in my drunken stupor.

"What's the problem?" I asked him defensively, presuming that he was probably overreacting to whatever misdemeanour I had committed. "You don't remember?" he replied in his thick central European accent whilst arching his bushy eyebrows. "You come home out of your mind, shouting this and that. And then you urinate all over the room and on me!" I was initially embarrassed, but couldn't help laughing. Thankfully, my antics did not shoo friends away. I gained more friends than I lost.

Despite my erratic behaviour on such occasions, I must have made a good initial impression because even during the training I was asked to manage a group of candidates from the YMCA. Eventually, I was being trained in how to use Steiner's range of Elemis and La Thérapie products, in order that these could then be sold to the clients aboard the ship. The oils, the weight-loss technology, other treatments and therapies...this was where Steiner really made its cut, so we needed to know everything inside out.

As we learned more about the various treatments and TV shopping-esque weight-loss technology, I felt a pang of uncertainty creeping in. Could I really sell some of these products? I was unimpressed but I knew I wouldn't rock the boat—I wanted this opportunity.

I was coming off the back of my transformation but I was able to maintain a level of motivation that I wouldn't otherwise have. My body was easing down from the brutal lengths I'd pushed it to in Pontypridd, nonetheless I felt great. There were times when I found myself drifting back to the pulsating experience of being in front of a crowd after my journey over those eight weeks. As the beads of sweat dripped from my brow while I pummelled the gym for the last time before the competition, drunk in a haze of happiness and faintness from my transformation, I knew it wasn't to impress the judges this time; it was about leaving a lasting impression on the staff of the cruise liner.

I broke myself from these reflections to try and focus on learning the various facial treatment techniques on the male practice models we'd been assigned. I did enjoy the feeling that I was progressing well. Well enough, in fact, that when it came to the end of the training a couple of weeks later, and people were sent home having not made the grade or waited to be put on a boat, I was thrown in at the deep end (if you'll excuse the pun).

Training was used to determine where the best candidates would fit in the Steiner world and I'd done enough not only to get on a boat straight away but to hit the mother ship: a celebrity cruise ship called *The Century* that would be going to the Caribbean. This was the equivalent of being picked for the A-team. The celebrity cruise ship meant opportunities for good tips and a high-end lifestyle. I was to join, initially as a personal trainer, in less than thirty-six hours.

I knew that you could be called at short notice (as little as twenty four hours in fact) but that doesn't quite prepare you for the actual flow of events. I flushed with pride once more and celebrated with my motley crew of room-mates and Jason. My parents rushed down to London to wave me off and collect some of my belongings I wouldn't be taking with me, including a petrol-driven electronic skateboard, called a Goped that I had been using to scoot around London.

Although it was sad bidding goodbye to my parents, the overriding emotion I felt was undoubtedly excitement. I was ready for a new adventure and while this wasn't my dream job, I hadn't yet worked out what was. And I was still reeling from my transformation, so I felt positive, confident and pleased that I was making strides after being stuck for long in a rut.

The reality of the cruise liner did not match my expectation, but I think deep down I'd always known the not-so-pleasant truth. Regardless, I was overjoyed to be getting such a great opportunity to start out in the wider world.

I began as a fitness trainer and was plying the trade that I would ultimately make a career from. But I soon realised that good money came in only if you were a masseur or in the beauty treatment. Our cruise was based in Fort Lauderdale but it would cover the Caribbean as well as parts of Central America which meant that there were lots of Americans on board and it was common knowledge that they tipped far better for massages than they did for fitness training. So with the hope of saving up a bit of money I switched my efforts to massages which began returning dividends.

The work wasn't overtly difficult and I soon came to identify my talent as a salesman too. However, it did feel repetitive and the days were long—normally twelve hours for six days a week. You woke up and had time for breakfast before you slogged your way through back-to-back appointments through the day with only a handful of short breaks. For somebody who was trying to maintain a healthy lifestyle and eat six meals a day, this was ironically sedentary work for a supposed fitness trainer.

Massaging is an intense experience, enveloping you in sound, sight and smell. We played those generic calming songs which certainly made sense to the clients but made me want to put the cotton buds in my ears. Especially on the 100th loop. Even today if I hear that music, it sends me into a swirling claustrophobia. Being boxed up in a room where you couldn't open the window because it let in the sound from outside in addition to the clashing music nearby, left me increasingly tense. Add to that, with people coming to cleanse themselves of negative energy day after day, you end up being the dumping ground. I was beginning to feel trapped and constrained. It didn't help to have a manager compounding that, either.

In order to try and keep up my diet I would slip many boiled eggs into my pocket at breakfast and gulp them down between clients. I would restock on protein shakes and bars from a local store each time we docked in Fort Lauderdale. It was a stopgap solution but I knew this arrangement couldn't be a long-term one.

The cruise liner bounced from island to island and port to port through the Caribbean and Central America. There was only one activity, that brought respite from the long, tiring and irritable shifts, the staff looked forward: hitting the bar after work. Initially, it began with one night a week to celebrate a good day at work. The frequency increased and eventually it became a daily escape from the monotony.

Bored from another day cooped inside a room with only boiled eggs for company I'd happily seek refuge in a drink or two. The beauty of it was that as a permanent resident you had a room card tab to charge on everything you wanted, vodka on tap and a bill that sucked only from your wages, not your pockets. And being in the middle of the ocean we were also living a tax-free lifestyle. The parties were fun and wild. I was slipping back into old habits. But I didn't mind—between all the hard work—I was having fun.

Each port opened a new world to dive into. I only followed my usual tactic: slip beyond tourist-grabbing locals flogging sunglasses and knock-off perfumes and embark on a quest for the hidden part of the island. A local bar, a jungle trail, a deserted beach, jet skiing, paragliding, diving across Jamaica, the Bahamas and Mexico...the list is endless. Every new place gives you a chance to learn more about diverse cultures, interact with people and, most importantly, have fun. During one of my escapades, I ended up on a nudist beach with a platonic girlfriend named Haley Heneghan who was, like me, a fellow therapist. These experiences helped me see the world for what it is, full of opportunities.

On 31st December 1999 we rang in the millennium, partying in the Caribbean with other members from the boats that joined us. The dark heavenly blue ocean, even under the moon and the stars, looked beautiful. Amid flowing alcohol,

I found myself trapped in hedonistic joy of being so far away from my previous life. As we ushered in the millennium at midnight, the party continued, thumping into the early hours of dawn. I cherished and revelled in the moment.

When I look back, I can clearly see everything that was wrong with it. I was allowing my old weaknesses to take hold of me, again. My body suffered, though not dramatically, because I was still doing my best to stick to my diet and exercise regime despite being consumed by alcohol. But there, in that moment, I was happy. And I don't regret the time at all. It was an important stepping stone onto my next chapter. It showed me the possibilities of travelling and it definitely taught me lessons about booze.

The source of agony was my manager who seemed desperate to crush my playful spirit. She would not miss any opportunity to put me down or throw her weight around only to win an argument. Whenever we pulled into port in order to prepare the rooms for new passengers, we had to do a thorough clean up. I do not shirk work so I'd make sure I went beyond what was expected to get the rooms spotless.

No matter what I did, she would invariably find something to pull me on. I remember this one time when, clearly frustrated that nothing in the room could be called into question, she climbed onto a chair and lifted the air vent shutter from the ceiling to point out the specks of dust on the blade. This level of exasperating micro-management killed me.

When I'm grappling with such situations, I turn to my own form of therapy—getting piercings as well as tattoos. I had taken them all off before going for the interview for Steiner, aware it was against the rules to have any on show. But I felt the urge to rebel, just to take back some element of the control that, I thought, had been sold to Steiner.

Safely docked into port I went to the nearest piercing parlour, determined, to get one done that wouldn't be on show. For the benefit of more sensitive readers I won't divulge more barring the detail that it was below my waist.

I returned to the ship, feeling good and relaxed. Piercing was my therapy, it gave me a release and reminded me I was real. As I climbed aboard I met my assistant manager, a girl who I got along really well with.

In the middle of the conversation, she gestured to my regular pair of white trousers—part of the uniform—the staff had to wear. We both looked in horror as a red patch appeared around my groin and the blood from my piercing seeped through the cotton.

Red with embarrassment I had to explain what the problem was. In hindsight the whole incident is funny to reflect upon but I was mortified at that time. Things only got worse (or funnier, depending on your point of view) when my assistant manager provided me with sanitary towels to help hide the problem, for it continued for days.

Despite the absurdity of the mishap, the piercing helped me to temporarily relieve the pressure I felt from my manager's borderline dictatorship. It was a decision I had complete control over and it prevented me from losing my temper with the manager.

I was also doing very well on the sales department. I had a knack for selling the more expensive treatments which in turn earned me more time off. It was, however, an example of why the cruise-liner mentality never quite fitted my scheme of things. My room-mate on the ship was a great guy called Sak Senyotkham, who was, on balance, probably a better therapist than me. But because I was good at sales, I was the one who got more time off. This jarred with my principles of hard work being rewarded; but it was a lesson in business as well.

Away from the therapy room and onshore antics I could enjoy myself in all sorts of ways be it theatre, live comedy, climbing wall, ice rink or cinema. It could be difficult to imagine a boring and a dry life on the cruise liner, but by the end of my journey on this ship, I was bordering on cabin fever. The late nights which were always oh-so fun sucked me in again and again.

Hunched over the bar with a group of equally bright-eyed friends, "Another vodka... In fact, get the bottle", would be— the inevitable cry—heard floating in the air. I would happily increase the size of my drinks' tab without worrying about the financial and health implications. Conversations bubbled and smiles stretched across faces.

Memories of these moments slipped away as the night sped up. Just one more, I thought, because we had to be up in a few hours. A semblance of sanity tucked at the back of my mind. Just one more.

Gin. Tequila. Another shot. Spinning into darkness.

Sunlight poured into a room of regret, bed sheet hung forlornly and the alarm shrieked. With the smell of stale vodka on my breath, I arose, resigned to yet another day of suffering. Shower. A beleaguered breakfast and back to the massage room, wishing I was still in bed.

This vicious cycle was a reality of the cruise lifestyle. Fortunately I had the sense to see and realise soon enough, that for all the fun I was having, it wasn't really leading me anywhere. The cruise was a honeytrap that I wasn't ready to fall for.

At the end of my contract, I decided I had to break away. It had been a great ride but it wasn't fruitful. I bid my adieus and hopped on a plane, this time, back to London to consider my options.

I made this journey with another guy from the ship, a South African from the casino, who was heading home. We landed in Heathrow and because he had a couple of days between his flights we decided to visit London. For once in the UK, the weather was glorious so we made our way to Hyde Park to sit beside the lake.

As we sat there, a gaggle of geese floated silently across the water reflecting the unusually blue sky. I looked up and it dawned on me there and then. I wasn't meant to be here. The blue sky and the pleasant June sunshine were a rarity, not the norm.

The sound of the city, the cacophony of traffic and the urgency were in the distance but still a recurring reality. Anyone who has ever been to London on a sunny day knows how impossible it is to escape the smog and the noise, even in the biggest parks. People swamp every patch of green and businessmen in suits occupy every bench in sight. When I'd decided to come away from Wales and the UK six months ago, I'd left this behind too. It wasn't me.

I remembered a poster I'd had up on my wall in Wales. It was when I had been working at the lacquering factory and had gotten into surfing with a friend named Paul Marshall. We had both bought camper vans and when we had a spare moment we'd ring up a shop in a small surfing town to check whether there was any swell. If there was we'd throw our gear into our vans and speed down there, rain or shine.

Surfing was freedom. With just swim shorts or maybe a wetsuit and your board you stand on the edge of the beach and feel the wind from the Irish Sea ruffle your hair and throw dashes of salty water toward you. Out in the waves, when you're with a friend, you're actually on your own. It's you, the board and the swell. Even on those days when you don't get the perfect waves, you come out of the sea feeling new and transformed.

The poster in my room was of the Bells Beach in Australia, the surf crashing onto the most beautiful shoreline I had ever seen. As I sat on that bench in Hyde Park, trying to isolate myself from the noise and admire the blue sky, I realised there was only one place I wanted to be.

5

Australia: A New Frontier

I didn't need to dwell on the decision. I immediately phoned an Australian girl I had met on the cruise liner. Colleen and I had been the two trainers who were trusted with the most lucrative therapy—Ionithermie—on the cruise. She was surprised but pleased to hear that I wanted to come over. We set the wheels in motion to make it happen as soon as possible.

Back in my native Wales, I began the process of applying for a visa to live and work in Australia. A few weeks and plenty of paperwork later, I was on a plane following the dream of the poster on my wall. From that day in Hyde Park, I never questioned the faith I had in my decision. I knew I was on the right path. I was ready to throw myself at this opportunity.

Unchartered territories intrigue me. The most exciting place in the world is the one you don't yet know. And that's what drew me away from the UK and toward Australia. Away from Terra Familiar and toward Terra Incognita.

Even from those very early days, scrambling through the woods in Builth Wells, I was always in search of something different and exciting. My parents supported me in whatever unusual direction I decided to take my life: from my beginning in bodybuilding through to the decision to quit my job on the cruise liner and head to Australia. And plenty more beyond that.

They actively encouraged me to push the boundaries of what others expected, even when I was at school. My very first piercing was an ear piercing that I got done at the age of ten. Far from doing it behind my parents' back, it was actually my father who accompanied me to get his done as well! I remember he'd gone in first and let out a howling scream. I'd recoiled in shock and fear of getting my own done, before he turned to grin at me and I realised he was only winding me up.

That's what my parents always taught me. Don't be scared of the unknown, embrace it.

In my decision to go to Australia, I had no illusions about the fact that I was taking a big punt. I had quit a well-paid job and the country I knew and loved (and still do); in favour of a land I'd never been to and had only met a handful of people from. The Australians I had met told me all that I needed to know. They were cool, calm, fun and laid-back. Australia enticed me to begin a new chapter in my life.

However, I hadn't anticipated what an ordeal the flight would be. My longest trip until this point had been the journey to Miami for the cruise, an eight-hour flight. However, the flight to Sydney from the UK is a thirty-hour flight with a stopover in Kuala Lumpur in Malaysia.

It's not that I hate the idea of flying—I'm relatively comfortable soaring through the air in a metal box. But being in a confined space for such a long period of time is a test of another kind. I couldn't bare it. I usually get bored on a long car trip, so I knew this was going to be agonising.

After going through the formalities of take off, I began to search for something to occupy myself with. I started watching one of the in-flight films to try and distract myself from the thought of the trip but I quickly lost interest and decided to get a drink. It had barely been ten minutes into the journey and I was already restless.

I had put myself in the aisle seat, as I always do, so that I didn't feel trapped, but even there I felt cramped—the seat didn't quite accommodate my growing physique. I positioned myself one way for five minutes before twisting and squirming to try and get comfortable in another. I must have been just as much of a pain for those around me.

I ordered another drink, and then another, in the hope that if I drifted off to sleep I might calm my increasing impatience. Slowly I began to relax and with the drink in hand I thought I might survive after all. I had a vodka and as the sun set on the UK I began to feel a little more positive, with a hint of anticipation for the land down under.

I closed my eyes and tried to ignore a man, two rows away, doing his best to drown out the sound of the plane's engines by snoring that echoed through the cabin. Finally, I began slipping into a drunken haze.

I woke up with a jolt as we hit turbulence. My head was thumping with a hangover. I called over the stewardess to ask for some water to take the edge off my dry mouth. As I saw her leaving, I hesitated to ask, "Excuse me, how much longer before we arrive in Sydney?" She looked at me, clearly confused, before replying that we'd taken off only seven hours ago—there were twenty-three more to go, including our stopover. Time was grinding to a halt.

I'm sure there are people who wouldn't find the experience anywhere near as harrowing as I did, but for me, being trapped in that space for the length of time, that seemed indefinite to me, was a personal version of hell. My only solution was to have another drink in order to kill time till we reached Malaysia, where I would finally get the chance to get off the plane, if only for a few minutes.

Over the course of the journey, I got drunk and woke up with a hangover on four different occasions: each time with an assumption that we were about to land.

It was a recurring nightmare. Posing the same question to the stewardess—Are we nearly there yet?—I felt like an impatient child in the back of the car. Alas, the time had barely moved forward since I last asked. Night turned to day and then back to night again.

By the time we landed in Australia, I had lost track of day and night. I was floating through the motions as I collected my baggage and made my way to the security.

If you've ever been to Australia or watched one of those TV programmes about border control, you'd know that the stringent security: especially for flights coming from Asia—as ours had—that included a stopover.

As I approached the desk, I was still reeling under the effects of my four-time hangover on the plane. To be honest, I was quite drunk. The stern expression on the face of the man I handed my passport to, suggested he was well aware of my condition. Perhaps unsurprisingly then, I was asked to open up my suitcase for inspection. The slurred Welsh accent was clearly enough to earn me a 'random' search.

I was an extrovert—I still am in my own way. And the contents of my suitcase affirmed that rather unapologetically. I often used to dress fancy, while having a drink with my group of friends, for fun. I loved being able to wear something a bit different, indulge in little eccentricities, and observe people's reactions to my 'absurd' sense of fashion.

In addition to my extensive bodybuilding kit and supplements, my suitcase also contained a hula skirt, a cape and an old-fashioned pilot's hat with goggles. The Australian border guard looked up at me and raised an eyebrow.

It must have looked rather strange, but, nonetheless he reluctantly waved me on. Nerves calmed and excited at the prospect of being off the plane and having safely made it through security, I began to plot some fun for my welcoming party.

I knew Colleen would be waiting for me on the other side, and my bag already having been opened, I decided to throw on the cape and the pilot's hat and goggles. As I made my way through the doors into arrival, I spotted her from a distance and decided to rugby tackle her in my outfit.

It all made sense in my head at the time. I dived at her, locking her to the ground in front of a shocked crowd. To begin with I thought I might have overdone it but a big grin spread across her face as she recognised me. Welcome to Australia. Welcome to Sydney!

Despite my dramatic entrance, I took my arrival seriously. Within hours of being off the plane (and sobering up) I was on the hunt for a job. I wasn't about to waste my money having a good time. And after that flight there was no way I was going through another thirty hours of it any time soon! I was here to stay.

Colleen drove me from the airport and we came to the Sydney Harbour Bridge. It was postcard perfect: the clear blue sky, beautiful sea and happy faces completing the picturesque landscape. Cutting into the skyline in the distance was the Sydney Opera House, with its roof jutting upwards like the sails on a boat, saluting the harbour's history.

I put my hand to my head and turned to Colleen with a smile stretched from cheek to cheek. Then with my head hanging out of the car window, I soaked in the sea air and looked below the bridge to see people rollerblading down the palm-fringed roads. It seemed I was looking at an artist's painting.

I was to live at Colleen's sister's place whilst I got myself settled. She lived in an area called Balmoral, slightly out of the centre to the north. Without wasting any time I started applying for jobs at gyms in the local area. Luckily, within forty-eight hours, I received an interview call for a role at a fitness centre called Bodyline.

The interview went really well—they must have observed how keen I was to make a good impression and land the position. It wasn't anything extraordinary to begin with and my duties included: clearing the floor, putting and arranging the weights and other equipments and generally helping around where I could. I was over the moon; I had a bit of security to underwrite my future in Sydney.

The present job was menial compared to the work I had been doing on the cruise liner. But it didn't matter at all, because this provided me the means to an end. Being on the ship, I was driving myself crazy, wandering and feeling like I was going nowhere; here, I got a chance to begin from scratch and Australia was my oyster.

The staff at Bodyline had amazing people. They helped me settle in. There's no denying that Australians do get a bit of stick in some parts of the world, but that only stems from jealousy. The (often misinterpreted) laid-back yet confident attitude teamed with a healthy outdoor lifestyle is responsible for giving the world some of its most talented and fit athletes from Australia. The incredible weather is a bonus. Hats off to these sportspersons.

My arrival coincided with the lead up to the 2000 Olympics and the place went even more abuzz at the prospect of showing the world what Australians were truly made of. It's pretty astonishing to imagine a country of just twenty million people consistently managing to produce some of the world's greatest runners, swimmers, cricketers and rugby players. Well, not rugby players—those are from Wales!

For me, the country was geared to healthy living. There's hardly anybody you'll find who doesn't love or follow a sport here and the attitude is competitive and infectious. They're confident and they're proud of it. They go in to win. This is commendable. Even if it does mean you're on the sore end of a thrashing from them.

The guys at Bodyline were no different. There was none of the nit-picking I'd been subjected to, by my manager, on the cruise liner. Their logic was simple; they wanted to have a good time and as long as you were willing to work hard, there was no room for complaints or unwarranted animosity.

In the business sector, the clientele mainly comprised people working in the city. Their attitude was to beat the traffic and get their workout in, early, before work. My hard work at the gym was appreciated and they acknowledged my worth by giving me extra duties that included locking up and opening up first thing in the morning. And lo and behold, at 5.30 a.m. people would be seen waiting outside, ready to hit the weights and treadmills. This was far from the casual afternoon sessions in the UK.

In they came, worked their arses off and hit the showers. All this before a day's work. I had been following a similar routine in Builth Wells during my transformation but it was such a welcome change to see so many like-minded people devoting their time to health and fitness day-in day-out. They kept coming in through the day, pumping iron and running until they had nothing left. If you want to see the Australian spirit in action, go to a gym. Then, head to a bar.

The Olympics gave me the perfect opportunity to get into the vibe, the Australian way. I managed to get tickets for several track and field events. Just like in bodybuilding, seeing those athletes in the flesh is an experience rather difficult to sum up in words. Being a Brit, I was also able to enjoy alongside the thousands of visiting fans. My sister too was also able to come over and join us in the festivities. I took her to the Sydney Tower restaurant, where despite being a vegetarian she couldn't resist the temptation to try their camel, snake, crocodile and even kangaroo meat.

A few years later, I would also get to enjoy the Rugby World Cup being hosted in Australia. I remember the swell of pride I felt gazing at the sea of red Wales' shirts flooding The Rocks in Sydney harbour before New Zealand played Wales. We were up at 37-33 during half-time and the atmosphere was nothing short of electric. In the end, the All Blacks came back to beat us but the match was unforgettable. Australia became a reservoir of precious moments and memories.

The final match, that year, was between England and Australia. And while I was gutted Wales had been knocked out by England, I can safely say, I had witnessed the greatest game ever. We watched it on the giant screen and at 17-17 in extra time, Jonny Wilkinson drop-kicked England to victory. Now that was theatrical.

I fell in love with Australia from the very first day and within a few weeks, Colleen and I became more than just good friends, and we started seeing each other. We decided to move in together. Her sister's place was only a temporary solution and now that I had found my feet at Bodyline, it was time to make a gracious exit.

When I and Colleen began house hunting, I had only one prerequisite. I wanted to live the postcard I had imagined before I came here. I wanted to wake up every day and live the reason for which I'd moved out.

We chose an apartment in Mosman, a bit more central than Colleen's sister's place where I'd been initially putting up. It was a great spot that pushed my budget right to the limit but there was one thing that made it worthwhile. . The balcony opened up to a breathtaking view of the harbour. And not just the harbour—the Harbour Bridge and the Opera House were also in full regalia.

I could watch sunsets, sunrises, thunderstorms, all through the lens of my recollection of the picture postcard moment and memory of my first arrival. And at New Year's, during the Olympics and the Rugby World Cup season, the firework displays were out of this world.

I needed to take on more work to afford the place and I grabbed almost everything that came my way. It started with tetrapacks—milk-based drinks that I promoted—handing them out as a sports drink (not that they were in any way useful). But I was game for anything that brought in a bit of money. From giving out Lindt chocolates (which had just been launched) to people on the streets, right through to dressing up in a fake-muscle suit and 1930s newspaper delivery boy outfit endorsing a Sydney-based newspaper, I did it all.

It might appear ridiculous to some, but I was determined to make sure I could keep the life I was living. My attitude is if you want something bad enough, you shouldn't let absurdities get in the way of your dream. You shouldn't be bothered by the kind of options you are presented with; you should only aim toward realising the bigger goal.

I was aware of the limitedness of my options and that they wouldn't sustain for long, so I started planning for the next few months. I upgraded my lifeguard qualifications at a place called Willoughby Leisure Centre. As a fitness advisor, this would professionally equip me to attract attention from potential paying clientele.

Eventually, I had to start my own personal training business. A few local clients would keep me busy during my breaks between shifts at the gym, at least for starters.

I got some rough and ready fliers printed out. I'd spoken to some friends back in the UK about recycling an already existing name for my gym to begin with, as a kind of ready-to-go branding. The yellow-and-black fliers might have looked rudimentary, but with 'Future Physique' and my name blazoned across the front, I felt confident.

During this whole time, Colleen supported me well. I was learning and focusing more on harnessing my abilities. I'd learned from the cruise liners that I had the knack of selling products, so I was taking something I owned and believed in (my skills) and offering it to people. It's a lot easier to sell something you're proud of.

Although I was leading a good lifestyle, I wanted to secure and build upon it. I might have lacked that academic edge at school but now I was doing something I had my heart in. At every given opportunity—from the cruise liner through to Bodyline—I was meeting and interacting with people I could learn from and expand my skills.

With what I felt was a good understanding of how to help somebody get fit, all I needed was the entrepreneurial spirit that I believe lurks in all of us. A risk, a jaunt into the unknown: I was ready to take the plunge again.

From the six months I'd spent in the area, I knew that there was money here. People were hard-working and knew how to earn. The one thing though they didn't have in abundance was time. So if I could bring the training and the fitness to their doorsteps, then I'd probably stand a chance.

As I trawled the streets, posting thousands of these leaflets, I knew I didn't need hundreds of clients—only a couple would suffice to make the effort worthwhile. Within a few weeks I had exactly that, four clients signed up in the neighbourhood whom I could comfortably manage with my other work.

In the world of business, nothing beats word-of-mouth recommendations. And every time I went to work with a client I gave them my undivided focus and attention. With the right attitude, I knew, word would spread quickly in the local community and I'd be able to add more clients to my list.

Slowly and steadily the number increased; four became six, which in a matter of weeks turned a dozen. At this stage, I could viably stop working at Bodyline and commit myself full-time to my business. For the first time in my life, I was running my own show. The feeling of liberation was overpowering and couldn't be underestimated.

Self-employment could be a short road to nowhere. If you're not ambitious, willing to take chances and self-driven—you won't be motivated to get out of bed each morning. But with the right attitude, of getting up before others, giving every client your best service and making sure you continue to grow your business, it's a blessing.

Meanwhile, I needed a car in order to not only run but expand my business as well. Up until this point I had been using my petrol-driven Goped to get around (as I did in London during the Steiner training). They were quite new in this part of the world, so there weren't strict rules governing their use.

I would travel between clients and fetch shopping for myself, but every now and again I would be pulled over by the police. Clearly, they knew there was something not quite right about a guy with six shopping bags hanging off the handlebars of a petrol-driven skateboard. With no laws over the dos and don'ts of its use, they didn't have a clue what they were going to charge me with!

They would just have a chat with me and then explain that they "would go and drive around the corner now" and "wouldn't be able to see whether I was carrying on my way." Clearly, they would rather turn a blind eye than go through the headache of working out the reasons for arresting me.

Add to that, I was a new entrant in the country and hardly on solid ground if I did get in trouble. It was necessary to change the mode of transport. So with a few thousand Australian dollars saved up I found myself a battered up, old Ford Granada in mustard yellow. I can't possibly begin to describe how ugly the car was—it was the Quasimodo of automobiles—but it fulfilled the criteria of having four wheels.

Compared to the UK where you could get a knackered old run-around car for the equivalent of $300, second-hand cars in Australia didn't come cheap. I was doing well to get anything for the money I had. And despite the dodgy colour I was now mobile which meant that I could get clients from further away and spend less time juggling Bodyline and Future Physique.

I decided to purchase a 'total gym' from my savings. Total gym was a mobile resistance exercise machine which I had seen Chuck Norris endorsing on TV. How can you say no to Chuck Norris?

It was a fantastic piece of equipment that combined lots of things you'd find in a gym into a single kit that could be used for dozens of exercises. It set me back a few hundred dollars though, but again it was well worth it. For the busy people of Mosman and Sydney, I was able to bring the gym to them (albeit in my mustard yellow Ford Granada). It created a whole new business avenue for me.

As anyone who has run a successful personal training business would know, the biggest limitation on your earnings is often the hours in the day. The Sydney traffic meant I had to time things perfectly to make each meeting possible and fruitful. One wrong turn or a flat tyre and your whole day could be screwed up.

After a few days of business, I once again started feeling that I needed something else to help me make more of my time and capacity. The obvious step was to begin taking groups of people instead of individual clients. Being so close to the city I was able to tap into the local businesses by offering my services to them. If I had the weather on my side, I realised I could also train my staff outdoors. Or else, I could also go for local hotels.

I would soon be completing a year in Australia and I was already feeling at home. Every step I took vis-a-vis my business was nothing but a game of trial and error. Sometimes, I would take on a new group of clients and realise I had stretched myself too far geographically. For every opportunity I grabbed, there was a slim possibility that another fell by the wayside. The key, when you're setting up your own business, is not to be bogged down by the failures but to learn from them in order to succeed later.

My DIY approach was fetching me good earnings and I was living a more comfortable lifestyle than when I had been scraping by for the last ten months. I still had to bust a gut every day, but the rewards were gratifying. Just a year in and I had built a successful personal training business. I was happy and I knew I had more in store.

Wales, 1975: Me taking a bath in a dishwashing bowl.

Wales, 1975: Enjoying the comfort of being in my Dad's lap.

Wales, 1975: Relaxing with Dad and thinking about my next mischief.

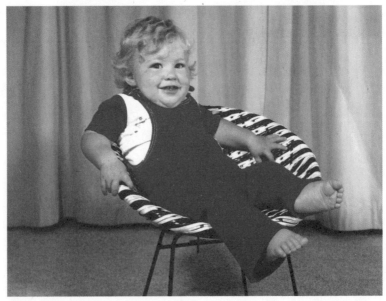

Wales, 1976: I knew how to pose for the shutterbugs from the beginning. I must be a little more than one here.

Wales, 1980: I cannot live without music. Playing on my drum kit. I am almost 5 here.

Wales, 1981: Practising karate moves at home gave me immense joy. I must have been 6 years old.

Wales, 1981: I loved to keep my hair long.
I am almost 6 here.

Wales, 1982: My penchant for cycling remains. Riding my bicycle at our farm.

(Top & bottom) Wales, 1982: On and around my parents' car in our farm.

Wales, 1983: Always on the lookout for adventure, that's me trying to climb a tree. I am 8 here.

Elan Valley Dams, 1985: With Dad and sister Ebonie. I am almost 10 here.

Wales, 1991: The thrill of racing catches on! During my first 2-Day Enduro. I must have been in my early teens.

London, 1998: Partying with friends and members of the Steiner team. We would all later be allocated to cruise liners around the world as massage therapists and personal trainers.

Llandrindod College, 1998: Surrounded by the Beauty Therapy students halfway through my complete body wax which I volunteered for charity.

Wales, 1998: Feeling a little worse after a holiday in Portugal. At home with friends Mark and Craig.

Fort Lauderdale, 1999: About to embark my first day on a cruise liner. Exhilarated!

St. Thomas, 2000: Kneeling in front of the cruise liner where I spent some of my most memorable days.

Sydney Australia Craft Market, 2001: My display of wood carvings that I sold on weekends while in Australia. I would do anything to stay busy and make a little extra money on the side of my full time jobs.

Sydney, 2002: A sticker advertising my mobile personal training business.

Los Angeles, 2007: With my adorable pet Iguana Zilla at my apartment.

Idaho, 2008: At home with (L-R) Chopper Jones, Marika Johansson and Neil Hill.

Tamarack Ski Resort, Idaho, 2008: With my lifeline, Mum and Dad.

Canada, 2008: At the Natural World Championship, Canada. I was awarded the first runner-up title.

Ohio, 2013: With good friend and trainer Neil Hill during Arnold Classic event in Columbus, Ohio.

Australian Bodybuilding Competition, 2003: Finished second, yet again.

Mumbai, 2012: With Neil Hill at Gold's Gym.

India, 2013: Conducting a practical training session with Neil Hill in a gym.

Seminar in Mumbai, 2014: It's always a pleasure talking to a bunch of youngsters. They are full of energy and enthusiasm.

Las Vegas, 2015: With friends at a pool party. Working hard allows me to occasionally play hard.

Punjab, 2015: During my visit to the orphanage. These girls have been an inspiration.

Boise River, 2015: Just chilling!

Golden Temple, Amritsar, 2015: Connecting with the spiritual side of me.

Wales, 2015: Shooting for the 4Weeks2Shred video series.

Boise, 2015: Filming one of my many videos for Bodybuilding.com from my home office.

Cape Town, 2015 : At a shooting range.

Africa, 2015: A friend's friend allowed me to get close and personal with a couple of crocodiles.

Wales, 2015: With my niece, Alys, at my parents' home.

Idaho, 2015: With Ryan Deluca, the CEO of Bodybuilding.com endorsing KAGED MUSCLE Supplements.

Idaho, 2015: Comparing biceps with my KAGED MUSCLE Director of Sales and Marketing Kate Kennedy.

England, 2013: With bicep curling friend and Ms. Physique Olympia Dana Linn Bailey during a photoshoot in Birmingham.

London, 2015: Prior to a KAGED MUSCLE
Supplements educational seminar.

Mumbai, India 2015: That's some serious weight lifting, err... Deadlifting!

Dubai, 2015: After a workout session, while on a Physique Global seminar tour with Ulisses.

Titan Gym, Sydney, 2005: Squatting over 700lbs. My training partner and Natural Mr. Olympia had to wrap his arms around my chest to keep my back straight.

Cardiff, 2015: During one of my practical workshops in Wales with the owner of Peak Physique, Dave (seen shaking hands) and my students.

India, 2015: With Jag and Ulisses on a seminar tour.

India, 2012: Training Bollywood actor Hrithik Roshan during the filming of Krrish 3.

India, 2013: With Bollywood actor, producer John Abraham.

India, 2014: With Chennai film star Arun Vijay at the launch of Gethin Gyms.

India, 2014: With actor Mahesh Babu.

Las Vegas, 2015: With friends Nick, Gary and Keith at Mr. Olympia.

(Top & bottom) Zambezi, 2015: Minutes before bungee jumping into Victoria Falls.

Uganda, 2015: On a hike to the mountains.

6

Australia: Building Body and Mind

After the first year of my stay in Australia, I found the time and also had the money to go on a holiday with Colleen. As is the case with most locals, she hadn't really explored her own country, preferring instead to jump on a plane to Fiji or Tonga. We decided to set this right by taking trips across Australia to see some of the incredible coastlines and of course, the Outback.

We didn't have the money to go jetting around the place, though, so we needed a way to bring the costs down. Coincidently, I had heard from a friend that rental companies would often have people rent a car or camper van in one place and drive it to another (for example, Adelaide to Sydney) without completing the round trip. The rental companies would then have somebody else drive it back for them free of charge so that they didn't have to fetch it for themselves every time.

This presented us with an enviable option to enjoy travelling for a bit less while living out of a camper van, just as I had dreamed of back in Wales. We struck a deal with one such rental company that we would return a KEA camper (one of those with a big roof that overhangs the front) from Sydney to Cairns—a 2,500 km journey—for just a dollar a day over ten days.

It was a long, old stretch but with the extra time in hand we were able to take a detour toward the coast. We spent days driving along the roads that disappeared into the distance because they were so straight. The Australian countryside is unique from anything else on this planet. Beside the many varied shades of desert and bush permeating the continent, the wildlife is everywhere—and there are animals you don't usually see in other parts of the world. From marvelling at the kangaroos keeping up with the pace of the car you're in, to gazing at the koala bears perched on the trees, we also had to obviously be careful about the free-roaming animals! I have to say I hated those crawly creatures that could creep up on you in Australia.

As we left the desert and bush and approached the coast, things turned greener. Towns came thick and fast and then grew sparser as we went north of Brisbane. Finally, after four days on the road with barely a stop in between we reached the Whitsunday Coast and made our way to the Whitsunday Islands.

The islands are just off the coast of Queensland and look nothing short of paradise. The shallow waters nestled between every size and type of island would melt any painter's heart. The sand is so fine that when you walk on it, the floor squeaks as though the specks were snow.

The water itself is every shade of blue, from the dark night sky through to a gloriously pale turquoise. Soaking up this beauty from our borrowed abode, it was hard to imagine anywhere in the world that I would rather be.

Admittedly, when Christmas came, I felt a pang of nostalgia for home. But when I sat on the beach, rubbing the fine dust-like sand through my fingers, I felt very proud of how far I had come in just eighteen months since I decided to transform my body and, consequently, my life.

The transition was apparent. With every phase of transformation that I underwent, I emerged more disciplined, energised and confident. During these trips too, I did not forget to have my supplements and food on time. Stability has been the foundation of my everyday life and that prevents me from giving into distraction or temptation ever.

I'd taken a few wrong turns along the way and had plenty to reflect upon. But I'd found a new life that I loved and an amazing companion to share it with.

Reluctantly, we set on the road toward Cairns, with still many miles to go. However, we couldn't resist but stop at the heartbreakingly beautiful beaches. As we made our way to our final destination, a series of mishaps began.

I had been sleeping and Colleen had taken over the driving. As I woke up, I went to use the bathroom and around the same time Colleen decided to overtake the car in front. I watched nervously as she tried to get any acceleration out of our huge camper van to get past the car ahead of us. We were approaching a bend when a truck flew around the corner from the opposite direction.

Colleen instinctively swung us back into the lane, narrowly missing the truck and barely keeping the camper van on the road. I had done my best to hold on but had been flung so hard by the swerve that all 180 pounds of me went careering into the shower door.

As I pulled myself to my feet and cursed Colleen for her reckless driving, I watched in horror as the shower door hung off its hinges on the $200,000 campervan we were supposed to be looking after. I rubbed my head and began worrying that it might not after all turn out to be such a free ride.

We continued onto Cairns and set about trying to find the place we were required to deliver the camper van to. This was long before the age of Google Maps and we were relying on sketchy directions to locate the rental parking lot in a city of 150,000 people. We approached what we thought might be the place only to find out it was a multi-storey car park for a shopping centre.

I was still trying to make sense of the map we were using and worrying about how we were going to talk our way out of the broken shower door. I failed to notice that Colleen had decided to pull into the car park to stop and ask for directions.

I looked up at the last moment to see the low roof sign disappear briefly above our heads before a loud screech forced us to a stop and the whole camper van judder as the roof was clawed from above.

Colleen had brought the van in with enough speed to wedge it under the roof of the car park, in the process taking the ventilation guard clean off the top. I watched in the side-mirror as it came crashing to the ground before settling in a crumbled heap. I put my head in my hands. Slowly I plucked up the courage to get out of the van and assess the damage.

As I looked up at the roof, clamped to the ceiling, a guy pulled up behind us. He leaned out of the window, looked at me as I inspected the van and said, "Hey mate, your camper van is too tall for the car park."

I turned to look at him, my jaw hanging open, not quite believing what I'd heard. My blood boiling, I thanked him for his thoughtful analysis of the situation by letting him know I was already aware. Well... I said something like that... but with a few more f-words.

I set about letting down the tyres on the van so that we could release the car park's iron grip. With that we were able to back the vehicle out enough so we could take a look at how badly we'd clocked it. It wasn't hard to imagine that a few small knocks could have amounted to a few thousand dollars, of damage, which we didn't have.

The scratches were deep and pretty extensive but we had one saving grace, they were limited to the very top of the camper van. Unless you were to climb right up, you couldn't see them. Was there just a chance that they might not notice if we played dumb, we thought?

With a bit of duct tape we managed to piece together, and then attach, what remained of the vent. It looked like it had been through a mangle (and then trampled upon by elephants!) but surprisingly the duct tape managed to hide the worst of it, unless you were really looking for it. Inside the van, some careful gluing in the scorching 40°C heat put the shower door straight. At least as long as nobody tried to open it!

Finally, after hours of searching, we managed to find the place we were required to deliver the camper van. We pulled into the car park to see an attendant slumped over the desk, clearly wishing he was somewhere else. I handed him the keys forcing light conversation and a smile. He seemed uninterested in even the formalities and for the first time I thought we might get away with it.

I watched as he climbed into the vehicle to take a look around, giving it a cursory once over. Then just as he looked like he was about to finish he began opening and closing the cupboard doors and making his way towards the shower. My eyes filled with panic and heart started thumping. But before I could try and distract him somebody shouted for him from inside the office. He turned to look over his shoulder once more at the van, shrugged and decided to leave.

We were in the clear and we rushed straight to the airport thanking our lucky stars we'd gotten away with it. It had been a hell of a trip though—unforgettable even. You'd think after our close run in we'd have thought twice about taking a van again. I might have been making a bit of money by now but I wasn't about to pay to replace a seventy grand camper van.

Sure enough though, a year later we were on our way to Alice Springs, this time, via Adelaide. A 3,000 km journey that took us to the heart of the country where we could visit Ayers rock, situated in one of the vastest deserts in the world, the sun beating down on our heads. It was a less eventful journey but almost as memorable for yet more breathtaking landscape.

I was quickly falling in love with the country but my business was still up to this point very temporary. I was living month to month and all of my equipment was pieced together and then dragged around Sydney. Although it was working I still yearned for something more solid.

That's the nature of the beast for any athlete. Victory and success is a short-lived sweetness. Then you want to go back for the next challenge.

The fire that had been ignited inside me during my first transformation refused to die. While I was working hard on building my business I was working just as hard on building my body. I felt good, but the only way I could put that to the test was through competition. I wanted to add more drive, structure and inspiration to other parts of my life. I knew a transformation would get me that—the competition was the bullseye I had to aim for.

It had been a couple of years since I had first set foot on-stage in Pontypridd. I hadn't enjoyed the experience in itself—the tan, the showmanship—I never felt wholly comfortable with the idea behind. But I did appreciate the sense of purpose that it had given me: the accountability.

I'd had to pull out all the stops with my training and there was no excuse at the end of the month if you missed a session in the gym. That competition was going ahead whether you were ready or not.

One thing that didn't change throughout this period was my passion for bodybuilding. I was still reading all the magazines I could lay my hands on, learning more about the sport and trying to develop my body to match the skills of the regular competitors.

Within a couple of months of arriving in Australia, I had already decided I had to give myself another goal to work toward. After my six months on the cruise liner, my body hadn't gotten much worse, but it certainly hadn't moved forward. I was stagnating and not taking advantage of the most important years of my life, physically.

There is more to it than just the physical. When most people see transformation photographs they are stunned by the physical change to that person's body. What you can't see is what it does to their mind. The dedication, the focus and the perspiration required can fundamentally alter your emotional and mental state. It makes you a stronger person, better equipped to face every challenge in life.

Before I could embark upon my next transformation, I needed some inspiration. So I went to a competition—this time, a natural bodybuilding competition for Mr. Australia. At the time of my first competition in Wales I didn't even know that there were drug-tested competitions, so I had stood shoulder to shoulder with guys not knowing whether we were on a level-playing field. It just didn't cross my mind.

I was amazed to hear that there were events that did check drug usage. I was even more amazed that it was serious. In Australia, the sport was quite developed and actually bigger than non-tested events, so the prestige was equal if not greater. When I found this out there was a flicker of excitement.

I wasn't a big guy but this was a way for me to compete and hope to win.

For anyone who has been to a natural bodybuilding competition would know that there is a big difference between the sports but the core principle remains the same: men and women pushing the boundaries of their physiques. There's quite a size difference, but the very finest, natural athletes blur that line. That's the beauty of it.

It was one of these athletes who blew me away at that competition. Mark Konstanti was guest posing and I couldn't believe my eyes. He was huge amongst all of the others there. His size, the symmetry of his physique and the body structure were unparalleled on that stage. Astonished, I asked myself whether he could really have that body naturally.

That's the sign of a truly world-class natural body builder. It's both a curse and a medal of honour. On the one hand, you will constantly have your integrity called into question. But that's when you know that you've taken yourself to a whole different level where you're so far ahead of the competition that the only way people can justify your performance is by doubting your integrity. If you know the truth and the tests prove it, you emerge a winner.

Mark was 100 per cent natural and drug-free and I was so bowled over that immediately after the show I went looking for him backstage. I wanted to know how he was doing it and what I could take back from him and learn. What I discovered, aside from the advice, was that he was a genuinely great guy. He could have brushed off the interest of this bolshie Welsh lad but he was happy to spend time with me. And before long, I found myself training with him.

At first we just did a few sessions together, and then I began to hang around the same gyms in the hope that I'd be able to pick his brain. Before I knew it, we were partnering up on a regular basis. I learned a lot from Mark during that time.

He encouraged me to enter another competition and I marked the date for Mr. Sydney natural bodybuilding event. It seemed like a good platform for someone like me and being tested meant that I had as good a chance as everyone there.

I should explain that I don't have a problem with drugs in bodybuilding. Many of my friends and colleagues use them in order to propel themselves onto that highest stage of competition. It's entirely their choice and for many it is a career-transforming decision.

The guys you see on stage are educated professionals who understand what they are doing, go through frequent blood tests and are monitored by health professionals to ensure they take care of their bodies. The dangers creep in when casual uninformed users try to use them as a quick fix.

From my own point of view, I had always wanted to see just how far my body could go naturally. And I think this is a good point of guidance for anybody considering that move— have you really pushed your body as far as it could go? Or is your dependence on drugs just a shortcut to your goals? I had become a little careless during that time. I was happily busy drinking and relishing my bacon sandwich instead of following diet rules like a competitive bodybuilder. My aim was to concentrate on eliminating these inadequacies before I even thought of progressing further.

Even after giving up alcohol and greasy food, I realised the jump from natural to non-tested was a huge leap. It wasn't for me. While I can fiercely admire the physiques of bodybuilders taking drugs from a distance, I wanted to push my body within the boundaries of the natural sport.

I enjoyed surfing, running, downhill mountain biking and later snowboarding. Variety makes me crave more opportunities. I didn't want to give up all of the agility I had purely for bodybuilding. The type of body you want is a choice all athletes have to make.

At my first natural bodybuilding event, the nerves were there again, but the experience was quite different. In my first show, I had been unsure of what to expect. This time I knew what I was doing. I had been concentrating on trying to build some body mass to make up for—what I perceived (rightly or wrongly)—my small physique.

As we got ready backstage, I looked around and was shocked to find, again, that I felt smaller than everyone else there. I've come to accept that this feeling, one I experience at every show, is purely psychological. I can look back at my photos from these events and see that I am bigger—but at the time, I just don't feel it.

This condition is called bigorexia and although it is treated with contempt, once I came to accept it, I've turned it to my advantage. I am never overconfident about my body which means I never fail to push it further and faster.

In the first natural contest, we went through our routines and I felt good and confident. Again, I made it to the final round. And again, to my disappointment, I finished second. Maybe there was a hidden point in it. To be so close and yet not have tasted victory was bittersweet.

It was frustrating but this was my first foray into the sport, so I could take it on the chin. I knew that I would take the right lessons away and come back stronger. I was still finding my ground in Australia and I was delighted with my work so far. Everything was very positive around me and I held my head up and got on with life.

My mobile training business had continued to go well through that year and the following one. But I wasn't content. And as long as I was confined to the day's limited offering of twenty-four hours, I could only service clients during that time. Not having a bigger operation was holding me back.

I was considering options to buy a gym of my own. It seemed simple in principle, if I had a gym I could delegate work to the employed staff and with a fixed base I wouldn't have to spend half my time battling the Sydney traffic.

I've always enjoyed scanning through the classifieds. Tucked away at the back of a newspaper or magazine you'd be amazed at the number of golden opportunities that you can spot with a keen eye. My father would always religiously browse through its pages, which is perhaps what I had inherited too. He would find all sorts from cars, to houses to bits of furniture—the entrepreneur in him could spot a deal.

On a break between clients one day, I was flicking through a local newspaper when I came to the classifieds section. And there amongst the usual mixture of second-hand cars and beat-up houses, was a gym. I was straight on the phone to find out the details and, most importantly, the price. That's what really sparked my interest. It was within my reach (at a push) and I began thinking I might be onto something. It's a step many fitness trainers take at some point—could this be mine?

My head swimming at the prospect I might have spotted my opportunity, Colleen and I headed over to the area the gym was in, called Granville. Colleen had already warned me that the location wasn't the best but for first impressions it seemed okay (though a considerable shift from where we were currently staying). It was drab suburbs, not a million miles away from where I had trained for the cruise liner. Dull but harmless, at least on the surface.

The gym itself was old-school; hard edged with no frills. It was plain and simple inside with doable, if slightly ageing equipment. It didn't exactly overwhelm me when I first walked through the underground parking and up through the reception but everything was in order. It was a fairly blank canvas and at the asking price (with a bit of haggling) I felt excited about its potential. I wanted to be positive about it. It felt like the right step.

Subconsciously, I knew it wasn't quite right. I was giving up the things I really enjoyed about my job—the flexibility, the freedom, the variety—in favour of a dream of owning a gym. A dream I wasn't quite ready for.

Reluctantly, we gave up our stellar apartment in Mosman, with that incredible view of the harbour. It still kills me to think about losing that. Instead, we moved into a place in Parramatta, near the gym that overlooked the river leading to the harbour, but didn't match the postcard image by any stretch of imagination. It was fine, but that's about it.

Good things come with a price tag or that's what my experience tells me. There are times when you have to make tough decisions and compromises in life. This was mine.

I placed my bet on the gym without any inhibitions. I was going to fight tooth and nail to make it work and I was upbeat. I knew what a good gym looked like and I made some simple changes to the look-and-feel to get it scrubbed up a bit.

The previous owners had concentrated almost entirely on the kickboxing department which I let be but hired some help to run it. That allowed me to get the other part of the gym off the ground again.

I stuck with what I knew and began leafleting the local area to drum up a bit of interest. This presented me with one of a kind experience as one of my firsts in Sydney, walking around a nice neighbourhood where money was on show. In Granville, the place had a feel of neglect.

The area had a bit of reputation as a dumping ground for immigrants, many of whom became regular clients. There was crime but more than anything it just felt different from downtown Sydney. It was a different city.

I hadn't realised quite how removed it was from my previous area, until one day I went to buy bacon for sandwich only to be told off with an unpleasant remark by the owner that they didn't sell bacon. I thought, "What kind of butcher doesn't sell bacon?" What I hadn't realised was that I had walked into a Muslim butcher. I would have to find someplace else for my bacon!

The people were good though and slowly but surely the gym gained some momentum. With members signed up I could begin to push secondary purchases with supplements and other extras. The cogs were turning and I could say I had my own gym, which was a source of great pride. But the spark was somehow missing.

One thing that was going well was my bodybuilding. I was gearing up for another transformation. This could give me the strengths to take hold of my new role at the gym.

Shortly before I got the place in Granville, I decided to take a break from alcohol and practise abstinence. I can't remember the day when I gave up drinking and proclaimed, "That's it, never again." I think I just slowly phased it out. I never had a problem with alcohol so I didn't need to go cold turkey. It was a simple observation and a realisation that it wasn't helping me go further with my body, so I cut it out.

With each of my transformations I took control of another portion of my life that I had been unable to previously— be it entering the world of bodybuilding or having the courage to leave Wales. This was my latest decision added to the list.

My tip to anyone looking to improve their body and physique is to learn about it from observation. Books and training can give you general advice but every person reacts slightly differently to different things. You can't expect one solution to work for all the problems. That's why one person can swear by a diet that does little for another. Watch your body, maintain a record of your diet habits and exercise and adjust accordingly.

Living in a country where drink and having a good time go hand in hand, my first two years in Australia weren't perhaps as consistently heavy as being on the cruise liner, but I was still partying most weekends. Watching my body, it became clear that no matter what I did during the week, if I had a few drinks on the weekend, I spent Monday, Tuesday and even Wednesday catching back up to where I was the week before.

It was like two steps forward and one step back. I couldn't make the progress I'd intended to amid such recklessness. Slowly, I began to ease back off to the point where without really making a conscious decision, I wasn't drinking at all. Despite this, it wasn't always easy and it meant I had to change my habits about where I went and who I hung out with. I needed to do it. I burnt a bridge so that I could build a new one.

The decision had an instantaneous effect. This was probably the single biggest impact on my body during my bodybuilding career. For the first time I was able to see exactly what my body was capable of if I really put my mind to it.

After the disappointment of my last bodybuilding show I was keen to build upon my stature. Entering Mr. New South Wales, the regional competition within which Mr. Sydney was part of, I was as big as I had ever been and I felt good. Having recently given up alcohol, I was confident this was my best chance yet.

It was a bigger and more competitive show but that's what I enjoyed. The challenge was what drove me through those twelve weeks of preparation. I felt as though I was getting the hang of things and niggle of finishing second in my first two competitions drove me even further. My bigorexia meant that I had pushed myself even harder.

It was not to be.

When I came second, for the third time in a row, and again by a miniscule margin, I felt crushed. I had played my cards wrong and not gotten quite lean enough. Perhaps it was just the nerves, but I was so close but not close enough. I was gutted.

I returned to the gym despondent. For the first time in my life my disappointment went beyond frustration. Being awarded the second position repeatedly was beginning to play on my mind.

I needed something new, an injection of something that could kick me out of this curse. I needed a transformation bigger than either of my previous transformations. One which could provide me with the mental and physical strength to decide where and how to direct the next turn in my life.

7

Australia: The Gym Journalist

At heart, I'm a bodybuilding buff. And my love of the sport continued to grow throughout my time in Australia, unhampered by disappointment on stage. One day I chanced upon some photographs by a guy called Robert Nailon. These were iconic images from the 70s and 80s of bodybuilding's formative years. I decided I had to have one for myself so I contacted him to ask whether I could get one of the photographs. Whether I had to pay for it or not, I craved that little piece of the authentic world I idolised.

He was unsurprisingly reluctant to begin with. After all, the beauty of photographs is that when you preserve them for yourself. You are unwilling to share the memories and moments that belong to you and are yours alone. Once you decide to part with your memories, they cease to be yours.

He agreed to meet me though and sure enough, once we got chatting and became more familiar with one another he warmed up to me. I was a bit star struck, not because Robert was by any means hugely famous outside the bodybuilding world, but because he could recall this golden era for the sport with a level of detail that nobody I had ever met could.

Robert would tell me stories of California that would make the hair on the back of my neck stand up. He had been close to

Arnold Schwarzenegger at the peak of his career. From Arnie's early years, right through to his seventh and final (and most controversial) Mr. Olympia title, Robert had been with him. His recollection of this weird and wonderful world would blow my mind. To browse through the photographs of my heroes from up close gave me a high.

The place where he kept the memorabilia was stacked to the rafters, not just with photographs but also reels of films. It was like walking into the biggest bodybuilding museum in the world with the best tour guide by your side, but with the knowledge of it being a private possession of a single person. And I was probably one of the fortunate few who had gained free access to this archival wealth.

Robert would tell me about nights-out with Arnie where he would operate the 'lamp test' on girls. The clubs would be dark inside and Arnie's theory was that you couldn't really tell whether a girl was good-looking or not in the gloominess. Best not to chance it! So you'd invite them outside to stand under a lamp where you could get a better look and decide whether to take them home or go fishing for someone else. I had to laugh at the outrageousness of this idea but at the same time I loved peeking into that world.

Ultimately, Robert actually gave me some pictures and photocopies from his archive. But what I took from him more than anything was a sense of what that time had been like—the culture. The bodybuilding fan inside me revelled at being treated to this glimpse into the lives of Arnie and others. I was invigorated.

I began to ask myself whether I would ever feel fulfilled without getting closer to the pinnacle of the bodybuilding world. Would Australia ever give me that?

Although I wasn't loving life at the gym as much as I had envisaged, I still felt at home in Australia. The trips out to the Gold Coast and into the Outback always floored me.

Colleen's family lived in the outback, several hours from Sydney, away from the city. That's where I loved Australia the most. I've never really chased after the luxuries of the city life. Maybe it's because I grew up in rural Wales but there's something about the traffic and the crush of people that tell me to get away from it sometimes.

Her father's house was a simple one, set amongst trees in the Hunter Valley; peaceful and quiet, save for the sound of the wildlife nearby. What impressed me the most was that he had built the place with his own hands. The timber that held the house together, the walls, the doors, the roof—every brick was his own work. His graft had made that place.

It was here that my subconscious decision to give up drinking was put to a real test. Colleen's father drank beer like most people would drink tea. It was a social thing and I could see why—what else would you want other than to sit on a porch in the heat watching the world go by? I could say no though, and part of that surely came from how comfortable I was in the place. It was like home away from home.

I could get up at the break of dawn to do my cardio and later jog through the bush. Nature feels more alive on such mornings. There were kangaroos everywhere. For an animal of their size, they are elegant, leaping through the forest barely making a noise. However, one of their weaknesses is their tunnel vision. If I stood absolutely still they could come within touching distance without even spotting I was there. So close that I could hear them breathing before they disappeared into the mix of bush and mist that hung above the ground first thing in the morning.

Colleen never understood why I liked to go out to try and catch the fox and lizards; or to watch the cockatoos. I didn't really think about it at the time but maybe it reminded me of home in Wales where I would run through the forests aged seven, hunting for rabbits. The place spoke to me. It was simple, raw and uncomplicated—and most of all it was beautiful.

Outside the house was a tin bath. Nothing fancy but it offered me the perfect place to relax and think about life. I would lean back and look up at the sky. Watching the single cloud drifting by above and nothing else would force me to seize the moment.

On one Christmas day, I sat out there when out of the corner of my eye I saw something move. As I turned, I caught sight of a tail slither between two rocks. Immediately, I lifted myself up to see more clearly. A long brown snake was getting close for comfort. In Australia, you don't mess about with snakes. Startled, I realised I was in a compromised position in the tin bath.

I shouted for Graham, Colleen's father and he came out running. Testament to the Australian no-nonsense attitude, he was carrying a golf club, a nine iron. He strode straight up to the snake and sent it flying with a hit that Tiger Woods would have been proud of. I'm not quite sure whether it was quite the right thing to do but it certainly solved the problem.

You had to give it to Aussies for that, they didn't mess around. Everything was black and white to them and you did what you had to in order to get along. In a land where the desert can swallow you up, deadly spiders crawl into your boots and you never know when the next drought, cyclone, flood or bush fire might be around the corner—you can understand that mindset.

So while I was dreaming of the golden era of bodybuilding, I was also in love with a place that was as far removed from that world as you could imagine. They were divergent paths and in 2003, I decided to take a risk on Hunter's Valley. Inadvertently, I was tying myself closer to my life in Australia.

In the late 90s, my father had sold our farm and decided to concentrate his efforts on real estate, where he saw an opportunity to make some money. This decision was partly the result of reading Robert Kiyosaki and his book series *Rich Dad, Poor Dad* which he would later pass onto me. He was brilliant at real estate and by this time in 2003, with the gym ticking over, I wanted to follow in his footsteps.

I saved up some money and with considerable help from my father and I took a loan to get a house in the Hunter Valley. I knew the area was incredible and while I wasn't planning to live there, I felt that buying property there would be a wise investment.

And it was. I was able to rent out the place easily and the money brought in covered the cost of the mortgage. It was a sound bit of business and I felt proud that I could put my name to a piece of property. Every stride I made felt like progress, though I still hadn't got a plan as to where that progress was heading.

One upshot to the gym was that I had a great deal more time on my hands. I could let people volunteer and do the administration that had eaten into my time with my mobile gym. I could concentrate on overseeing the place and on transformations which I continued to do myself.

I believed that only by providing the best to a client would I be doing myself justice as fitness trainer. And every person who went through a transformation was a walking advertisement for our gym and my training. There was no way I was going to delegate the task to anybody else. As a result, while I might have had more time to explore other avenues, I was still working around the clock to make sure clients were happy.

You can't underestimate the power of a good transformation image. When we were first starting out at the gym, one of my leaflets was picked up, from a fish and chip shop, by a guy called Matt. He gave me a call and asked if he could be my first transformation client at the gym and twelve weeks later he was in phenomenal shape.

The jump—from fish and chip shop chump to magazine cover Adonis—was evident in the photos we took and we were able to use them to drive more and more business. These pictures were our product, they showed what we were capable of offering, which is why for all the clever words and marketing, it's often the before and after shots that matter the most.

Despite my constant involvement in the transformations, between clients, when I would have otherwise been stuck in Sydney traffic with my mobile gym, I had time to try out something new.

One of the reasons that I had bought a gym in the first place was that I wanted to reach out to more people, and help them transform their lives. It worked, but it wasn't anywhere near the audience I needed.

I had been reading bodybuilding and fitness magazines since I was in my teens. Apart from seeing the incredible images and being inspired by them, it was about visualising the competitions moment by moment without being physically present.

The Internet was fast becoming the next big thing but to be honest most of the bodybuilding world still existed outside of it. If you wanted to know what was going on, you had to read the magazines. Which is why, when I was in Wales, I would harass the newsagents to give me the latest edition before anyone else.

There's a special skill required to bring a bodybuilding event to life in print. The pictures only tell part of the story:

the rest has to be done with the written word. This was long before webcasts or live videos, (other than for the very biggest events) so you had to rely on the writer to help you relive the moments. And through their words about the superstars you found motivation to push yourself further.

I remember reading Peter McGough, Editor-in-Chief of *FLEX* Magazine and Alex McKenna at *Muscle News* and admiring the way they could light up the page with their descriptions. What made them stand out from other writers was the dry wit they possessed.

Articles which could have been run-of-the-mill were given a new colour by their ability to spot the little thing that would make you laugh. Bodybuilding can be an incredibly intense and serious sport—if you can bring humour whilst retaining the gravity of your writing, you have got something special. These were the guys who inspired me to start writing.

I had absolutely no background to fall back on, given my complete disinterest at school. And I had no pretension that I was going to be any good at it. But the very idea of having a platform on which I could encourage other people to pursue transformation in their body and their life spurred me on.

It probably started with some newsletters that I was doing for the gym. I was learning as I went along and although I didn't possess the skills to brighten up the page like those whom I looked up to, I did know and understand bodybuilding well. I could give insight and share my knowledge that others might have lacked. That was my advantage.

Then I bumped into Gary Phillips, Editor of *FLEX* magazine, Australia. He was originally from Leamington Spa in the UK, so I got chatting with him as a fellow ex-pat. He must have been sufficiently impressed with me because when I chanced my arm to ask if I could contribute to the magazine he said, "Why not?" I'll never forget that opportunity Gary gave me.

The first article I wrote was on a local up and coming bodybuilder called Luke Wood. I got his contact details and invited him to come up to the gym for an interaction. I was finding my way and winging it. I interviewed him and to my astonishment the article was published. That's when it clicked for me, the rush of seeing my name in print and knowing all those people were reading my words.

I started off fairly slowly, writing an article once every month or two: first for *FLEX* and later for magazines like *Beef* and *Body Fitness*. I would report on events, write general articles about transformations or interview bodybuilders—whatever interested me, I could pick and choose.

When I look back on my earliest writings I think, "What on earth was I doing?" Because I was still learning the basics about writing and no doubt the editors had to do a great deal to bring my articles up to a certain standard. That's part and parcel of throwing yourself into something new. You can't be too proud to make mistakes or admit you have more to learn. Otherwise, you'll never improve. I had no doubts that I was finding my way in the dark, so I continued to read more and more to expand my understanding of writing and the sport.

When the opportunity knocked on the door to go to the U.S.A. with Gary, I grabbed it. *FLEX Australia* needed somebody to cover the Mr. Olympia event. Had they asked me to cut off my right arm for it, I wouldn't have batted an eyelid. I was spilling over with excitement and anticipation.

When I arrived in the States I could finally see the dream life I'd been idolising since I first read those magazines back in Wales. California is everything you see in the movies and more: the beaches, the people, the buzz, the glitz, the glamour.

Exactly as I had when I arrived in Australia for the first time I tried my best to soak it up but was overwhelmed by the whole experience—it was a breath of fresh air from life at the gym.

In Australia, I'd become trapped in a monotonous cycle of my own making. The gym was going well, making money and bringing in clients who appreciated my efforts. But every single day was exactly the same. I would wake up, see the same faces, in the same places and do the same things. Only my writing allowed me to break away from this mundane rhythm.

While I was mobile training and focusing on many transformations, the people I worked with and where I worked were constantly in flux. It lacked stability but at least it was exciting. At the gym, I had lots going for me but I'd lost the spark that had attracted me to the land down under in the first place. And my place in Hunter Valley was beautiful but I had no intention of living there. America's allure was instant.

In Los Angeles we visited Gold's Gym, which for the fan boy in me was like visiting one of the Wonders of the World. Training on the best equipment, catching glimpses of athlete after athlete and absorbing the reality of being at the very centre of the coveted industry, thrilled me no end. This was where it started and here I was—the lad from Builth Wells.

When I attended the event all I had to do was report each and every action on the field. That meant a couple of hours' work after which I could enjoy the events without worrying about meeting deadlines or editorial targets.

Mr. Olympia is held in Las Vegas, Nevada, the state inland from California. Set against the backdrop of Death Valley on one side and the Grand Canyon on the other, the lights of the Las Vegas strip are like seeing a fairground for the first time as a kid. Swirling neon colours intoxicate you before you've even got near a bar.

The weekend I was there it so happened that Tom Jones and Marilyn Manson were playing shows in Las Vegas. I couldn't go, obviously, but it opened my eyes to the fact that America really is the centre of the world when it comes to entertainment and sport.

My first hit of reality came when I went to the press conference. It dawned on me that I was actually reporting the Mr. Olympia—this colossal event. I wasn't being paid (yet) but this investment could well be a precursor to something more rewarding in the future. It was another risk but one that was fuelled by my latest transformation and an increased hunger to take on bigger challenges. Things became surreal as I listened to the Mr. Olympia MC, Bob Cicherillo, drumming up the ante between the competing bodybuilders. These legends were in a tussle with each other right in front of me.

Günter Schlierkamp had been playing up his chances of beating the title holder Ronnie Coleman in the lead up to the competition. And as things began heating up, in the press conference, he leapt onto the table to strike a pose. Almost instantly he was followed by Ronnie Coleman and, not to be outdone, other favourite Jay Cutler. It was like watching your favourite film stars acting out a new scene in the flesh—the drama, the entertainment and everything else felt surreal.

Mr. Olympia is for the hardcore bodybuilder fans. It is a world where those few competitors are the single point of focus and no corners are cut in making sure they look their absolute finest up on stage. I wasn't just watching from a distance, I was backstage; I was talking to the athletes. And I was beginning to realise these were my kind of people. Focused, dedicated and hungry.

Six months later, I was on another trip from Australia to the States with *FLEX*, this time for the Arnold Classic. It was an excruciatingly long flight, which was delayed in Chicago but worth it, nonetheless. In the freezing March temperature of the Mid-West, I was about to have my world turned upside down.

Arnold Classic is huge, to begin with. I mean massive. The venue is always full to the rafters with thousands of spectators queuing up to watch these titans clashing against each other. I was wandering around like a kid in a candy shop. After the first day, I went back to my hotel with a suitcase full of free supplements. Scattered across my bed, I felt proud of my haul and made sure I took a photograph.

The Arnold Classic's also not confined to just bodybuilding, there are more sports on show than at the Olympics, so there's a diversity attached to the concept. That also means it loses a bit of the 'purity' of Mr. Olympia but the first time you go you're too gobsmacked to notice or even care.

Most importantly the place, the venue and the event have a sense of occasion and showmanship which will blow your average Joe away. It draws in such a range of people that the focus on bodybuilding is lost, but only by a whisker. The bodybuilding event remains the centrepiece.

Participation in the event is invitational and only fifteen candidates are allowed to compete. As I sat down to watch and file my report on my first live event, I couldn't get over the lights and lasers that flooded the stage. It detracted a little from the bodies of the athletes but for the audience it was phenomenal. And then came in the pyrotechnics. Flames ripped upwards from the stage puncturing the tense anticipation in the air as the crowd went hysterical. The effect was theatrical.

While I spent a lot of my time devouring it as a fan, I was even luckier than that. With a backstage pass I could see and talk to the very biggest names in the industry from Dorian Yates to Dexter Jackson and Jay Cutler.

There is a particular 'Meet the Olympians' session where fans and journalists speak to the athletes and the first hour is reserved for the journalists only. But rather than using that privileged hour for interviewing like I probably ought to have been, I was storming from table to table like a kid getting autographs and taking photographs. I was still living in a dream world.

Prior to the final I stood backstage and watched on as the competitors took off their tracksuits. This was the moment when we would get a glimpse of what would be on show. Who would have turned up looking that bit out of shape? Who would reveal a chiselled back in phenomenal condition?

It was there and then that I knew I had to do this job for a living—the rush of being this close to the action was unparalleled in my life thus far. I was desperate to share these moments with thousands of fans around the world like myself.

It wasn't just my bodybuilding idols that I met for the first time. The most important thing to have happened to me that weekend or in fact on any trip to America was when I met this person.

I was with Gary again and he introduced me to *FLEX International*'s Editor-in-Chief Peter McGough and photographer Kevin Horton: two of my idols of bodybuilding journalism. Before I knew it I was drinking with them at the bar, talking about the day's events.

It turned out that Peter and Kevin could seriously drink and the conversation flowed as thick and fast as the booze. Kevin would get us shots and follow it with a beer chaser. The night spiralled and I joined in caught up in the moment. I wanted to live this life and I would do whatever it took.

After talking to Peter I made it my mission to get myself published in *FLEX International* when I returned to Australia.

And over the next few months I would regularly write articles, sending them to him in the vain hope that I would hear back from him.

Despite getting no response I stuck at it, occasionally receiving a note saying thanks but no thanks. It would take more than that to stop me though. I'm persistent to the core when I want to be.

There's only one phrase that comes to mind when I try describing the joy of speaking with stalwarts, Peter and Kevin, and seeing those stars up close: life altering. I was trying to keep my cool but the fact was I was in paradise. Not only was I meeting these guys and shaking their hands, I was there in the capacity of a reporter. I had taken a leap into the unknown once more and I was flourishing.

Only later, when I would attend and write and report on such events for Bodybuilding.com, my perception would have undergone a change. The 'heavenly' seemed 'ordinary' and 'normal'. I was there to work but the work was easy enough and I could focus on being a fan. In fact, the article I wrote for FLEX was titled, 'Diary of a Bodybuilding Groupie'. I wanted to share with the bodybuilding community what it was like as a fan to go backstage.

I returned to Australia feeling as though I'd taken a shot of adrenaline. I had witnessed glorious moments and now I wanted the glory to be fixed to my name. I wanted to be the owner of what I truly deserved in my bodybuilding career. I set about putting myself through the most intense training of my life. I had been building myself up for some time now and mentally preparing for what was to come next.

8

Mr. Australia

I'd first been to the ANB Mr. Australia to see Mark perform, just a couple of months after landing in Australia. It had been a revelation that had inspired me to enter both Mr. Sydney and Mr. New South Wales. I was gearing up for the nationals and with no alcohol, no shortcuts and a much greater body mass, I felt good. I had worked for five years for this opportunity.

At the same time, on a sadder note, things were starting to fall apart with Colleen. I like my independence and I believe that for a relationship to work you need to be living two lives—it keeps you interested in one another and it gives you the space to miss one another. Over the years we'd become almost too close and my heart was no longer in it.

Colleen was after something I couldn't have given her. I felt smothered and my time in the States had offered me a view of another world. It happened over a long time but we grew apart and eventually decided to call it quits.

In turn, that inevitably meant the gym and the house I had bought in Hunter Valley no longer felt like possessions of pride. They were weighty iron shackles around my ankles that I couldn't shake. The monotony of life at the gym was thrown into sharp contrast by the Arnold Classic and Mr. Olympia trips. I began to understand that I was at a crossroads.

It would take something drastic to force my hand though. I had built up a life in Australia, could I really give it all up to chase another dream?

With the big day approaching, those thoughts had to be shelved, at least temporarily. During the build up to Mr. Australia I had the blinkers on—with my eyes firmly on the prize. I had actually made the decision to compete nearly two years before and had been working up to it since then.

Seeing my idols during my trips to the US had sharpened my focus and when it came to those twelve weeks of transformation I was ready to put myself through hell to be ready for the show. I had seen and felt inspired by the giants on the big stage. The chance to lead my sport nationally was a draw but, as always, I was driven by my love of the journey. Those twelve weeks were my therapy and my reward, the competition was necessary but transforming my body was the real prize.

It's difficult to put into words what the gym and pushing my body means to me. One of the few people who ever captured the feeling was a guy called Henry Rollins, who as well as being a writer and radio host was the lead singer of one of my favourite early bands, Black Flag. He wrote about the truth that 'The Iron' gives you in life. When everything else is chaotic around you, it is The Iron that can shut it out, give you perspective and understanding. No matter what kind of day you've had when you face The Iron, "Two hundred pounds is always two hundred pounds."

These words mean so much to me not just because I enjoyed the music he helped create but also because they explain so simply why bodybuilding is more than just a physical sport. It is therapy for the body and the mind. When you are alone on the machine or with the weights, it is easy to isolate yourself from the busy world full of discord. You can see yourself for who you are.

The journey to transformation is a long one, but it is also as much about those individual moments along the way as it is about a start or finish. When you reach your absolute physical limit, the final rep that seems to be tearing limb from limb, muscles flooding with agony and your mental strength kicks in and hurls you forward once more, the sensation is inexplicable. The intensity binds you with the machine entwining your fates.

It's in this space that I reach a state of contentment. My faculties drive me to nothing else but how many reps I've done and the faith that I will keep going. When every ounce of strength has been poured from one part of the body, I'm onto the next, safe in the knowledge that I'll be back and I'll be stronger than ever. It is my therapy that cleanses, empowers and fuels me.

The journey is the highlight; it is why I strive in the first place. But I also seek the end of my goal, the competition, to give me accountability for my journey. So when the competition begins, it bears the weight of all the work I've done. This is what matters; it's not really about where I finish but examining whether the results reward me what I have earned. 'Second place' had ceased to do that. The very idea of 'second' was beyond me now.

At Mr. Australia, I went through the same anxiety pangs as always. Glancing around, I felt the pangs of uncertainty that clouded my mind. Was I big enough? Was I lean enough? The answer was emphatically 'yes' according to those there to support me but as always I couldn't see it when I was in the moment. I shook off the doubt and focused on preparing my tan and running over my routine once more. The pressure borne of my three second places in a row hung over me like a dumbbell chained to my neck. I would have happily taken third place to avoid the pain. Just not second, anything but second.

As expected I was declared one of the finalists. I took to the stage and made that same eye contact as I did in my very first event, demanding that this was my time. This wasn't Pontypridd though and the prize was much, much bigger—as was the competition. The lights were blinding, cameras flashed and faces stared. Before I knew it, it was results time.

As always, the names came out in reverse order and as we approached the final three I felt my chest tighten. Dread surged through my mind and every bone in my body screamed, "First or third... but please, not second". I resisted the temptation to close my eyes and turn away and instead kept my gaze fixed to the ground.

Fifth and fourth places came and went. And then third. Still nothing.

And then, finishing second is... "Kris Gethin."

Again.

AGAIN.

Surely, this had to be a dream or was this some kind of a joke?

I felt numb, my hand trembling as I attempted to steady it. But my stomach was churning with the injustice. Not that I hadn't won, but that I was being awarded the one thing I couldn't stand.

I held myself together, never once looking up at the guy who had beaten me or the judges who were punishing me. I couldn't make eye contact, just like that day when I went to see the friend who had been sleeping with Suzie. Except this time the anger wasn't directed at anybody. It was swirling inwards, punishing me for finding myself in that same place again.

That day brought some of the most hurtful memories I wished never happened. To compound things people kept coming up to me to say I should have won, that I'd done enough. That was the last thing I wanted to hear. All I could do was nod and smile. My mind was foggy, thinking about the months of work it had taken to reach this peak but I searched for something to make sense of it all. I was furious and broken at the same time. Two years of building up to lose it by an inch. Again, it was a single point that had done me in.

Ultimately, bodybuilding is a subjective sport. The slightest gut feeling that a judge might have, whilst looking at you, often sets the difference between the first and the second rank. I just happened to have been on the wrong side of that line four times in a row.

I wondered, was he bigger than me? Leaner? More symmetrical? The subjectivity crept into my mind and gnawed away at my self-belief. But when I looked back at those photographs of the event, I felt even more deflated. Objectively—as an onlooker like I had been in the US—I couldn't reconcile to this failure. I was in phenomenal shape.

It couldn't be put down to anything other than bad luck. That was something I hated more than anything. On that day, it felt as though no matter what I did, how much I prepared—it wasn't in my control.

I started to think about control and the power I'd worked so hard to have over my life. More than anything, it hurt to think that for all my efforts, stubbornness and sweat had not resulted in what I'd hoped for. That wasn't the way I viewed the world so I didn't want it to be true.

Admittedly, I was happy that I had gone through the transformation and completed yet another phase of my ever-expanding journey. I had used it to propel my life forward and give me greater perspective and understanding of my own place on this earth. Ultimately, even the competition had its benefit because it caused me to reflect deeply upon where I was going.

I had to fight back and start getting rid of the shackles I felt were holding me down. I put the gym and the house up for sale. I was at least a bit disappointed to let the place in Hunter Valley go. That was and still is one of the most inspirational places I've ever been to. But it wasn't where I wanted to be, so it was only a burden.

It took several months for the gym and the house to sell. And by the time I finally managed to get everything together, things had really come to a dead-end in my mind. I'd grown weary of the day-to-day drudgery in Australia. It had ceased to inspire me the way it had been for the last five years.

My head was in a different place: Venice, Los Angeles to be precise. I had yet to secure any work with *FLEX International* but the signals I was getting were positive. I had been sending in pieces which were consistently being rejected but I had developed a good rapport with the Editor, and Gary Phillips who had introduced me to Peter McGough persuaded me that it was within my reach.

The truth was that I had to take another risk, this time on my ability as a journalist. If I was ever going to do it as more than a part-time project I simply had to be near the Mecca of bodybuilding. I had to be in the US and I had to set out to L.A.

The work I was doing for Australian and other national publications was frequent enough to pull in a little money but wasn't sustainable independently. I knew to some extent I would be able to fall back on my skills as a fitness trainer but in the land of fitness and health would I find the work as readily as in Sydney?

In addition, I hadn't given up on my own bodybuilding career by any stretch of imagination, despite the heartbreak at the nationals. I was confident that given the right goal and a fresh start I could go even further. I was without doubt in the best shape and I knew I had more in me.

As a measure of this, two days before I departed, Gary and I had been out in Bondi for an alcohol-fuelled send off. The morning following, head hurting (remember I hadn't been drinking regularly for some time now), we had a photo shoot lined up. I was supposed to be squat lifting 700 pounds for it, a colossal amount by almost any athlete's standards.

The gym, Titan Fitness, owned by two bodybuilders named Mets and Murat and one of the very best gyms I've ever visited in the world, was one I regularly worked out in. It had become a talking point in the gym and amongst the bodybuilding community which reached Gary's ears. I would become so engrossed during the hour of warming up for these heavy sets that later I would look up to see most of the gym had stopped to watch me.

So Gary and I had agreed to do these shots but with my hangover it seemed a little unlikely. Nonetheless, I entered the zone of concentration and focus that I had become adept at creating for myself. An hour later, I was ready, and to mine and Gary's surprise, considering the drink, I managed it.

I left Australia relying upon my savings and my faith in my own ability to become a journalist. I never gave a great deal of thought to the long-term plan: my focus was on getting what I wanted as quickly as possible. The sensation I had at the Arnold Classic and Mr. Olympia, the rush of being part of the pinnacle of my sport, and being paid for it, was enough to pull me to any part of the world.

The part of the world I had to go to was Los Angeles: City of Angels—from Hollywood to basketball, the Universal Studios to Gold's Gym—the original and best of everything in the entertainment world. It is exciting, intimidating, exhilarating and daunting at the same time.

I learned that I would have to graft. There was no job waiting for me. Would I end up like so many others, eaten up by promises than never materialise? I had no idea but I guess that was part of the attraction: the danger.

I could only afford a very small bedsit. It was simple but I didn't begrudge paying for it. I was more interested in what was outside—in the sun, on the sidewalks, on the beach. I was living close to Gold's Gym, Venice: the very first, original and still the centre of the bodybuilding universe.

Venice was modern and yet trapped in the 70s. Everywhere you looked there were murals of famous artists—like Jim Morrison—or the houses formally occupied by film and music stars. The past hadn't been entirely relinquished, but the radiance of the 21st-century lifestyle was unmistakable. Never had I been to a place before where the energy was as contagious.

Surrounded by freaks that lit up the city with colour and life, I felt inspired. During the day it would burst with skaters, rollerbladers and surfers. And at night it transformed into a carnival of musicians and vibrant culture. It was impossible not to be seduced by the place.

In my room, while I worked on an article, I could hear the buzz of this rebellious and bohemian city, see the festival of colours and smell the wafting joss sticks as they permeated the air. The smoke would rise from the streets below, softly scenting the air with the sweet odour of the Orient. That smell is a fond memory because my mother would use the same sticks at home in Wales and the nostalgia would wrap around me like a warm blanket.

I felt instantly at ease in Venice and I continued to develop my writing skills. Meanwhile, I also purchased a Canon 40D camera. I had gotten myself a cheap camera while I was in Australia, on the basis that it allowed me to write articles and provide pictures, greatly improving my offering.

I had grown up with the sport, reading every magazine I could lay my hands upon so I knew instinctively which shots would work and which wouldn't. It was only a matter of trial and error to get the hang of how the camera functioned and despite the relatively low quality of the pictures; I was still able to sell my articles because I was coupling the images with my writing.

In contrast, the Canon 40D, was an investment. It was a proper kit that in the right hands could produce professional shots worthy of an international magazine like *FLEX*. Gary Phillips showed me how to use it and imparted the tricks of the trade which would unlock the power behind the camera.

Today, a digital camera does most of your work. But it was still important that I knew what I was doing. Armed with it I could both attend and report an event and provide pictures from the show. This alone allowed me to get the work I needed to tie me over, writing articles for *FLEX Australia* and others.

The most important thing was my location. I was in the international hub and I was training at its Mecca. For those who have never been, Gold's Gym Venice remains, fifty years after it opened, the place where everyone from Mickey Rourke to Hulk Hogan to Charles Glass (Michael Jackson's trainer and the best bodybuilders in the world) could be spotted. Add to that, the countless professional boxers, wrestlers, bodybuilders and other athletes that frequented the place.

Most days, I would be in Gold's Gym and it was here that I really thrived. Not only could I see the greatest athletes in the bodybuilding world but now that I had met many of them through Mr. Olympia and the Arnold Classic, I could approach them. And soon I become good friends with many of them. Once I got over being star struck, I bonded with several over our shared love for the sport.

Dorian Yates's was perhaps the greatest friendship I forged during this time. A year earlier I had greeted him as a fan, getting his autograph and purchasing pictures from his booth in the expo hall at the Arnold Classic. Now, a year on, I was lifting weights with the six-times Mr. Olympia champion.

I fiercely admired his attitude towards his bodybuilding. There are few people I have ever met who are so intense. I respected him for his unmatched passion for the sport. He was warm and generous with his advice. We've remained good friends ever since. And it would be Dorian who would provide me with my very first *FLEX International* article.

Gold's Gym has always provided free access to bodybuilding professionals. Nothing drives business like having the biggest names in the sport frequenting your gym. That's how Dorian had been going to Gold's in Venice, for many years, without ever having to pay.

Once when we were entering, he was stopped by a member of the staff who said that Dorian needed to pay for his time in the gym. Dorian explained that over twenty years he had never paid to use the gym as he was a pro. "Ah," the member of staff replied. "Well I'll need to see your pro-card." Dorian shrugged and said he didn't have one and had never been asked for one.

Clearly feeling more confident the guy challenged him, "Well, how do we know who you are then?" Dorian pointed at the picture behind the staff member's head and said, "I'm the one in that picture, where it says six times Mr. Olympia." By this point I was laughing my guts out at this guy's misfortune—needless to say the picture put the issue to bed.

I jumped at the opportunity to share the anecdote with the guys at *FLEX*, and after a few hours and a little editing, I had my first content. When it went to print I got a bit of stick from the manager of Gold's for making the inexperienced member of staff look out of his depth – but frankly, that's exactly what he was. Don't work in Gold's Gym Venice if you can't recognise Mr. Olympia winners... It was well worth it, and I didn't look back from that moment.

I felt motivated like never before. My body was evolving and my diet and eating habits were impeccable. I was the little fish that had been thrown, not into a bigger pond, but into a raging sea. All around me were these monsters of towering men. I was out of my depth in every way imaginable but rather than drowning, I found myself thriving and striving to grow further. The challenge of training with guys twice my size would set my heart racing like never before.

I had left Australia in search of a jump-start—something new that would motivate me to get up each day and awaken the hunger in me to reach the zenith. I had bitten off a great deal more than I could chew but between my existing journalism assignments and a couple of personal training clients, I had held my fort at all junctures. And now that I was steady, I had the structure in place to propel myself toward the bigger target.

9

An American Dream

It was during my early days as a journalist for *FLEX* that I met one of the most important people in my life: Marika, my future wife. I was starting to get into my stride with my writing. I was being published on a regular basis by *FLEX* and my growing number of contacts at Gold's Gym and elsewhere meant that I had my foot firmly in the door.

Being so close to the action, the opportunities were coming thick and fast. Rather than writing and reporting from a distance, as I had in Australia, here the athletes came from all over the world to my doorstep.

Marika was an up and coming female bodybuilder and preparing for a competition to be held in Texas. She was training in Venice. On behalf of Bodyfitness, I went along to do a shoot and interview with her. We started with the shoot on the beach followed by the interview at the Max Muscle store, a place that sold supplements and also great hang-out zone for bodybuilders.

Thanks to the equation I shared with the owner Dave Bourlet, he was extremely helpful and let me interview athletes on a regular basis. He was also generous enough to introduce me to a lot of bodybuilders who frequented the place. It was the ideal place to interact with bodybuilders as the relaxing atmosphere helped them open up and often give me the information that made the best articles. That was key to my limited success; whether I was training with an athlete before a competition or just hanging out with them, I'd built a rapport with these sportspersons that in turn helped me with my writing. You can't underestimate the importance of making somebody feel at ease with you as a journalist.

In Marika's case, our meeting was quite low-key. I remember being struck by her positive outlook and gentility. As professionals, women bodybuilders often have to bear the brunt of gender stereotypes. They are perceived as 'masculine'. Perhaps, such judgements stem from their being within the territory of bodybuilding and muscle-making. Bodybuilders are considered physically imposing. And certainly, physically, Marika was big—she was in training for the biggest competition of her life, after all. But her femininity was far more apparent. She seemed soft, genuinely kind and good-natured.

Things were entirely professional at this stage but I remember being filled with a sense of wonder at Marika's earthiness. This was her big break. She was from Sweden and this was her first competition in the US. Despite the daunting nature of her first big competition she seemed confident, relaxed and overwhelmingly positive. It was her honesty and positivity that made her stand out. She did not have the over confidence that I had become wary of in Los Angeles, where everybody is busy trying to put their best foot forward to the point where they are falling over one another.

We kept in touch after our first meeting. She did well at the competition in Texas finishing fourth and over the next few months she was back in Venice again to compete and to attend more events.

At Mr. Olympia 2006, we met for the third time and finally things started to click beyond the professional ambit.

I began to realise just how strikingly beautiful this blonde heroine from Sweden was. I was an admirer of her beauty and compassionate character.

In the years prior to our meeting, she had to put her career on hold in order to look after her mother who lost a battle with cancer. Her inner strength was both powerful and warm. I couldn't help but be drawn to her—amid all the showiness and glamour of bodybuilding, Marika was refreshingly honest. She loved the sport in the same way that I did and shared my passion of seeing bodybuilding as a pursuit of something much bigger than success in competitions.

Thankfully, she saw something in me too and around that time we began seeing one another. Over the next few years, she would continue to grow as a strong influence in my life, her positivity helping me to push forward—this time as a team.

The beginnings of my relationship with Marika and my time in Venice was tough. I had given up all of my safety nets and, while I wasn't living in poverty, I had to run a tight budget to get by. Even my modest apartment proved too much of a stretch as time went by and I was forced to look for something more economical.

In comparison to Sydney, rent in Venice took a big chunk of my income. And whereas in Sydney I could move to another area to save money, the very reason I had moved here in the first place was to be not just close to the action, but in the thick of it. Living it. I couldn't afford to give that up.

I had to prioritise. My bodybuilding and time at Gold's Gym cost me money but it was both my passion and in essence my bread and butter. On the one hand, I was living a pretty frugal life at home but on the other, I was spending my time alongside the rock stars of bodybuilding.

Once things had steadied out and my income from FLEX and other writing became more regular and reliable I decided

I needed to do more than simply get by. In the hope of saving up a bit of money I traded my own place for a shared flat, this time with another bodybuilder.

It sounds like a brilliant idea in principle—given that we were both living similar lives—you would expect that it would make things easier. The truth is bodybuilders aren't easy people to live with. Each has their own structure and way of going about things which can't be impinged upon. Put two together and rather than cancelling out each other, it only makes things all the more difficult.

I was living with a bodybuilder named David Hughes who shared my passion for the sport. Living together wasn't easy though—we were on top of each other. It was a really meagre existence given how well we were both doing. Dave was focused solely on his bodybuilding, demonstrated by the fact he didn't have a single plate in the house—only Tupperware for his food.

Dave was a really laid-back guy, soft-spoken but always up for a laugh. We would meet each other at Gold's, grab post-workout pancakes at the Firehouse restaurants and often attend bodybuilding events long after we stopped living together.

The flat we shared was so small that in order to fit all of my stuff in it, my bed was raised an extra foot off the ground. Add Marika to the mix and to say we were short on space is an understatement. Despite the fact David had been featured on magazine covers and had a supplement contract, Marika was a pro athlete and I was now writing regularly for an international magazine, we had to scrape a living by in the industry. For all the celebrity and allure of bodybuilding, even on the fringe of the big time you have to work really hard to have a modest living. That's the reality behind the splendour seen at competitions.

None of that really mattered to me at the time. I had grown up as a fan. To be even making a living (however modest) was a dream come true. During my days on the cruise liner my only drive had been money, or securing extra time off. By the time I was in Venice I was so happy about being able to live my dream that the money came a distant second to knowing that I was at the centre of the bodybuilding world and actually beginning to make a name for myself.

It was in this context that I hit a real break with writing. I had heard about a guy called Flex Lewis who was making waves, having come over from the UK after winning the British title whilst still only twenty-one. What was more, he happened to be Welsh so when we bumped into each other one day the connection was almost instant.

As it happened, he had also heard about me and when we met by the lockers in Gold's Gym we recognised one another straightaway. To see another Welshman in Venice was rare, but to see a person of Flex's calibre and reputation was extraordinary. Immediately we hit it off and spent time training with one another. It was great to be able to reflect upon the surreal and exciting bodybuilding world with somebody from my own neck of the woods. Flex's talent and potential was frightening to be around.

Over the next few months we spent more time together and one day I came up with an idea for an article. Flex was new to the scene but his successes hadn't gone unnoticed. This made me wonder, Could a British bodybuilder seriously compete at this level for the biggest prizes in the sport? There was only one other person in recent memory who had done so, the six-time Mr. Olympia, Dorian Yates.

With this idea I put the suggestion to Peter McGough that we might do a feature on Flex coupled with Dorian. Peter was intrigued by the idea enough and told me to go for it. Dorian and I were good friends by now and I asked him whether he would be interested in doing a photo shoot and feature with Flex back in the UK. He was up for it so we agreed to meet back in the UK.

Flex and I met in Wales along with Flex's mentor, IFBB Pro and former British title holder, Neil Hill and drove over to meet Dorian in England. For my article I described in detail the anticipation of the journey as we wound through misty country lanes. For the shoot we played upon Dorian's legendary back which had lifted him to the titles during the 1990s. Flex was shot doing shoulder weight training, in effect the master and the apprentice. We captured the moment perfectly, these two goliaths together, muscles bulging and veins popping.

I felt both excited by the article and immensely proud to be showing off a fellow Welshman on the international stage. What I hadn't imagined was just how well it would be received by Peter. A few days after I'd submitted it I got a call to say that not only were they running the story, it was going to be the leading article. Dorian was featured on the front cover accompanying Flex's name. For Flex, this was an enormous break. He was flung from breakthrough starlet to global news alongside a giant of the sport.

I was delighted for Flex but I was equally pumped for myself. I had barely been writing for a matter of months for *FLEX International* and I had achieved what dozens of writers never would, a front cover. And not just any front cover—one which celebrated my home country and an extremely exciting talent and friend. My gamble in moving to Venice had forged this opportunity in its entirety but my growing ability to spot and create an angle had seen it through.

The rush when I saw the magazine in print was phenomenal. I was flung back to my days when I had begged the newsagent for the latest issue of the magazine. Who would be in this month's issue? What pictures would adorn its jacket? Somewhere somebody was going through that exact experience and it would be Flex Lewis' image that they would see – my article and photo shoot was reaching the lives of people all over the world.

That prediction, that Flex was on the edge of something huge would eventually be realised. And in 2012 and 2013, Flex was crowned Mr. Olympia for the 212 category, after a decade of support and training from another fellow countryman and friend, Neil Hill. For three lads from a tiny, cold and wet but very proud country, Flex's achievements were an immense badge of honour.

The front cover was a once-in-a-lifetime opportunity and the true highlight of my time with *FLEX*. I had found my opportunity and struck gold. The question remained whether I could do the same in my own bodybuilding career. It had been a couple of years since I had last competed but I had an even bigger opportunity at my doorstep.

My time in Venice had seen another enormous shift in my body's evolution. Physically, I was around guys who were much bigger than me, hugely so. Rather than reeling under the defeat in Australia, I had gathered myself up being in the midst of such great talents. My desire to raise and push myself to their level spurred me on and I took this as a challenge. Alongside my work for *FLEX*, my body had developed from strength to strength and I was in the best shape ever. It was while working at Gold's Gym, with giants like Dorian and others, I came to a happy realisation that my body was favourably responding to changes; instilling me with the confidence to strive for the unattainable.

Besides my good fortune of training with the best, and on the best equipment in the world, my diet in Venice was impeccable. I had easy access to the best nutritional supplements in the world and the place was geared up to the lifestyle of a bodybuilder. It was far easier to maintain the diet I knew I needed. I had fine-tuned the nutrition my body demanded and was regulating my meals like clockwork every day.

Consistency is at the heart of any professional bodybuilder's diet. Prior to going to Venice I had to work extremely hard to build that into my life. It all began whilst I was still on the cruise liner. I made a commitment that I would not miss a meal—not by accident, not as the result of a crisis, not for anything. I would consume at least six meals a day, rain or shine. That would rise to eight in the lead up to competition, no mean feat.

It sounds quite simple in principle but the reality of a commitment like that over the course of years is that no matter where you go, who you are with, what you are doing—you have to be prepared to take out a Tupperware box with your pre-prepared meal and eat. From those earliest days where I would sneak eggs between clients on the cruise liner, I had to forcibly engineer time to make sure I got my meals and kept up my diet. It was the only way I could guarantee I would continue to grow and maintain the body I had. I didn't have genetics on my side so I had to fight for it. I had to have absolute control.

There were countless occasions where I could have slipped up. In my time in Australia I was still drinking and partying but no matter what I was doing or how far gone I might be, I would get my food, pulling out a protein bar with a pint of beer in my other hand. I guarded that record with every ounce of my being. Not once did I let up.

Even when I got very ill in Australia and could barely keep my food down, I found a way. I fashioned myself a tuna and tomato soup which I could just about manage and lived off entirely for days on end. After several years of fiercely maintaining my record I wasn't about to let being ill snatch it away from me.

By the time I was in Venice I had not missed a meal in five years. As I write this, I haven't missed a meal in sixteen years. Consistency and dedication became entwined with my very existence. The idea of letting it slip was unimaginable. I don't even think about it.

You can go to some outrageous lengths to ensure you get your meals. But if you are serious about it you need to be prepared. There's no other way to protect yourself from the crises that can pop up at any given moment and mean that you can't get the food you need.

This simple decision has helped me indirectly in so many areas of my life. It has enabled me to live my life with confidence and discipline without giving in to excuses of any kind. It has allowed me to control my environment, my life and my future instead of being controlled by the world around me.

Later in my career, as a reporter, I would attend the Arnold Classic and barely be able to get a moment of rest, such was the intensity of the work. Writing, reporting, interviewing, editing, organising, presenting awards meant I couldn't spare a moment to stop and think, let alone feed myself.

To battle this, I arrived with forty-seven pre-made meals all in Ziploc bags, ¾th of them frozen in a cool bag until I got to the hotel. At the front desk I told the receptionist that I was diabetic and needed a fridge for my insulin so that I could store them. Once again airport security must have thought I was crazy, with this arsenal in my luggage. But it was necessary— it was how amongst all of the chaos I could ensure structure. Structure was integral if I wanted to get back on that stage.

Since I had left Australia I had remained in touch with a guy called Ron, who was responsible for the Australian Natural

Bodybuilding Federation. He was interested in finding out what shape I was in since I had departed the land down under. He recognised just how close I'd come in Sydney and how difficult missing out on the nationals had been: the crushing blow of coming second for the fourth time in my career and by a single point, again.

He knew that I had continued to build upon where I had been at the nationals. He also understood how much I had wanted it and how I had lost out by the slimmest of margins. Against this backdrop he threw me the opportunity I had been waiting for (but certainly not expecting). He invited me to compete on behalf of Australia on the international stage, at the Natural World Championships in Canada.

For all of the disappointment I had suffered in Australia, there was never any doubt in my mind that I would say yes. A chance like that only comes along once and while my passion for writing was growing, it was still founded upon my love of bodybuilding. This was the chance to reach the very top of the sport that I had dedicated the last seven years of my life to.

It's difficult to put into words what being asked to represent a country in the sport of bodybuilding means. On the one hand, I had never meant to reach that stage; it had never been my driving force. From the day when I had huddled in the warmth in my car in Pontypridd before my first event through to that event in Canada, it was a by-product of the journey I was on.

Even in Venice, where there were so many others vying and trying to get their chance to grab a title, I had been pumped up by the impact the transformation of my body had on my life. Not by any hopes of glory.

But at the same time, it mattered and it mattered intensely. I had been given the chance to put to bed each and every one of those heartbreaks in Australia. And on the biggest stage at the Natural World Championship.

I had a little over nine weeks to prepare to represent my (former) adopted country and I went through yet another brutal transformation to get myself into shape. The event was to be held in Toronto and the mixture of nerves and fatigue from the weeks of preparation was daunting enough before I had even seen what I was up against. This was a whole different level to anything I had come up against before, I had no idea whether I would stand a chance or be completely blown out of the water.

I had grown to accept that with the territory of pushing the limits of natural bodybuilding comes the possibility that you'll be asked the question. And in the pre-competition warm up, when judges were asked to single out potential cheats I faced exactly that. The judges told me that they believed my physique was not that of a natural athlete. Despite the fact I had no signs of gyno or distension they believed I was using a growth hormone.

I felt my heart drop out of my stomach. There is nothing more gut wrenching than having your very integrity questioned. To have come all this way, to have battled so hard to protect my diet, to have watched as others used drugs but to have stayed true to my decision not to—those words were the ones you didn't expect to hear.

The physical transformation I went through came with immense mental strength too. And despite hearing these challenging words I knew that I had to take the positive from this. If they believed that I couldn't be a natural athlete, I had to be in great physical shape. I had achieved my ambition of reaching that line where natural athletes approached those taking drugs. Amongst the pain of being accused, I could feel a swell of pride that all the sweat and tears had been worthwhile.

I underwent a polygraph test as well as the normal drugs tests which confirmed my innocence. With my honesty back intact I could now look the judges square in the eye and know they couldn't question my integrity. I was going to stand shoulder to shoulder with the international competitors, flown in from around the world.

It was in this heated and intense moment that I got the shock of my life. Coming off stage from a preliminary round I ran into a face from my past. The last time I had seen Jason St. Marie was shortly before I embarked upon my cruise in the Caribbean. We had been, briefly, the best of friends during our training in London and here we were, nearly seven years later, backstage of an international bodybuilding event.

It turned out that Jason was competing in another category at the same event. For the briefest of moments I was thrown out of the focus I had engrained during the previous nine weeks of build up. I was back at the cusp of my decision to leave the UK and explore the world.

As quickly as I was broken out of my focus I was jolted back into it. Over the tannoy, the next weight class was called and I remembered where I was. Jason and I agreed to catch up once we were on the other side of our respective challenges and I returned to the changing rooms to try and calm my nerves.

I climbed onto the stage for the last time, my body pulsating, throbbing even in the harsh lights that would have shown up the slightest hint of any excess fluid or muscle weakness. I was pumped and as I struck my poses I could feel my body trembling, so tensely was I straining my muscles. Veins bulged and my body shimmered as I prayed for a release from the build up.

As we were lead onto the stage that glimmer of hope had crept in again. I was starting to believe once more but I was to be left sprawling once more.

It seems incredible to even say it, but once again my name was called out in second place. On this highest of all stages I had yet again come within a hair's breadth of victory only to have my hopes dashed. The first placed loser, again. I could barely believe it.

Every single time I had entered a competition in the last five years I had found new strength, new energy and new belief. Yes, the nerves remained still when I was on stage but the sheer consistency of my defeat was impossible to stomach. I felt shattered to the core. How could something like this keep happening, why was I being given the one rank I couldn't stand.

For the first time ever I questioned whether I should give up. I couldn't imagine standing on a stage again and facing the possibility that I would have my dreams crushed once more. It hurt too much. My stomach sick and empty and any enjoyment I had garnered from the build up drained completely. I returned to Venice. From the World Championships to disaster, where could I go from here? How could I start anew?

I sat on the side of my bed, wedged up by belongings. My head was held in my hands and my heart pounding in my chest. For all my work, the risk-taking, I had been left in pieces by something I'd never set out to achieve. The glamour of Venice, *FLEX* and Toronto had taken me to a giddy high but what was I left with underneath it all.

I felt a pang of self doubt shoot through me. What was real? I went to the only place I found solace at these moments of hurt: the gym. I battled my demons the only way I knew, by blocking it all out and searching for the one thing that can never be questioned, my physical limit. I pushed the iron until I had exerted every drop of energy from every muscle. Drenched in sweat and breathing heavily I returned to my room dejected.

The rush of having my first magazine cover had subsided behind a growing resentment at the extent to which my articles were being warped and changed. When I began I understood that I was learning the ropes and I was grateful for the direction but now I felt shackled and unable to express myself in my writing.

The principle upon which I had grounded myself—integrity—was foundering as I watched photo shoots that used fake weights or manipulated surroundings. What was wrong with the cold hard reality of the gym—the brutal honesty of where ninety per cent of people worked out on their own, pushing their personal boundaries?

I still adored the world of bodybuilding, it was one I had worked my life towards being a part of but I couldn't stomach the way in which it was being portrayed. Flaky, false and superficial. I wanted something more and the difficult nature of my rise and fall in Toronto showed me that. I wanted to return to my roots and give Venice a piece of who I was and what I really believed in.

10

Kaged Muscle Unleashed

I never grew tired of the bodybuilding world; I just believed it had more to offer. My burning desire has always been to help as many people as possible learn about how their body works and how they can take control of it and their life. With *FLEX* I had a platform available to me using which I could reach out to hundreds of thousands of people around the world and encourage them to understand their physiques and bodies through and through. However, I couldn't help but feel there was something missing.

The tipping point came whilst I sat at the bar during the Mr. Olympia show with Dorian and some of the other athletes. Mr. Olympia is probably the event that's most true to the sport; it has never compromised or over stretched itself. It is the real deal for the bodybuilding world. Everything that you saw at the event was for the benefit of those competing.

At the event, I had received a signed copy of Joe and Ben Weider's book *Brothers of Iron*. It had struck a chord with me, telling the story of these two Jewish kids who in the depths of The Depression had started their own magazine from scratch that had revolutionised the world of bodybuilding. They were in many respects its founding fathers and were responsible for the sport I grew up loving. I wanted to see this replicated in the publications that reported on the sport in 2004. One that shared the Weider brothers' passion.

I was now writing for a diverse array of print and online bodybuilding publications. But I still felt that there was a gap for something more honest and truthful. Something that'd cut through all of the hype and remind people what it was all about: physical and mental transformation. It was about taking control of your life by taking control of your body.

Talking to Dorian and others at Mr. Olympia, I explained how frustrated I had become at the industry for misconstruing the message to one of vanity over substance. The fake weights used in photographs, the manufactured backdrops that had nothing to do with the sport. It was doing the athletes who busted their balls every day to stay in shape a disservice. The real story was interesting enough to stand on its own feet. So why wasn't it the one being featured in the magazines?

If I had my own magazine I could share the true message. I could show the athletes with honesty and away from the pressures and controls of editors who had to push a certain supplement or agenda; away from all of the politics and the dishonesty with the freedom and control to create really great content.

"Why not?" I was asked. First Dorian and then others told me wholeheartedly that they'd love to be involved in getting a new publication off the ground with content. Despite the fact I had no experience of anything like this, they trusted that I could create something that would do them justice.

At first it seemed unlikely and I wondered whether it would go beyond the promise of support from my friends but then I realised that having talked it up I owed it to those who had backed me to follow through. And off the back of my failure at the World Championships, I needed something to pour my energy and resolve into.

Once again, a transformation had given me the power to take on a new challenge in my life. Certainly, there was disappointment from the competition but the bigger impact was the new found surge to have, hold and own something that I had created.

With the small amount of money I had saved up during my time in Venice, I took another plunge into the unknown. I managed to find a second-hand printer, for a couple of thousand dollars, that I could squeeze into my flat (Marika and I were now living in our own place). That was the first vital step and one that meant that there was no turning back.

I was finding my way in the dark again, from sourcing and creating content through to the design and layout of the magazine. I was guided purely by the belief that I was doing something worthwhile that would give me an outlet for my frustration at what I saw as failings from the traditional publications. I planned to do what I'd always done—work it out as I went along. If you spend all your life worrying about how you'll overcome each challenge, you'll never face up to them. Better to throw yourself in at the deep end and sink or swim.

I was driven by a desire to create a magazine that would be read by athletes and fans alike. Something that would focus solely on the sport I loved: bodybuilding. I was focused and gathered inspiration from the gym I worked in.

The name of the magazine was to be called, *Kaged Muscle*, in honour of the emotion I associated with my bodybuilding. A sort of an alter-ego that I'd adopted when I worked out, an outlet for my anger, anxiety and frustration. *Kaged Muscle* was the inner resolve that powered me through those final reps when my body had all but given up. It was something I recognised in so many athletes in their intensity and dedication beyond the normal limits that most would be prepared to reach. It was a place and a person that I turned to when I wanted to be distracted from the chaos.

I was bearing my soul in publishing under the title, *Kaged Muscle*. I was ready to give my all in this venture. Within a matter of weeks following Mr. Olympia I had found numerous people to help contribute to the magazine. I wasn't about to fill the magazine with odds and ends—I wanted to land with the best I had to offer.

The fact that I could even entertain the idea of creating an entire magazine was the sum of the last few years in Venice; I knew the athletes—I was friends with many of them. I knew the gurus, the nutritionists, the retired stars, the up and coming new faces and they all trusted in my love for the sport. They were happy to help me out.

In addition to Dorian, I recruited a guy called Dr. Nick Evans to provide medical advice as a regular feature. That was at the core of what I wanted to achieve with the magazine: real advice, not pseudo science, which would provide useful information to readers.

The list of names that contributed or were involved in that first magazine would have made any bodybuilding publication proud. I had a Q & A with the eight times Ms. Olympia Lenda Murray, an interview with Catherine LeFrancois and a retrospective with Bill Grant looking back at the Golden era of bodybuilding including when Mr. Olympia used to held at the Brooklyn Music Hall. We coupled the features with on the ground news about Gold's Gym in Venice and the Mr. Olympia event where Jay Cutler had finally wrestled the crown from Ronnie Coleman.

There was also a piece by Rick Welling that aptly conveyed the message I wanted to spread through the magazine. Rick was a pro-bodybuilder who had overcome being blind to become a phenomenal athlete. Through the sport he had found a way to not just live, but to thrive.

It took all the energy I had to fling together the various articles in the few weeks I gave myself. Marika helped to design the magazine and by the time we had everything together, one late night in November 2006, I was physically and mentally exhausted. Would it work? Would it be worth it? I had no idea.

It was 1 a.m. but I wasn't going to sleep until I had the complete article in my hands. I rubbed my bloodshot eyes and shook my head which was spinning from having poured over every single word trying to spot mistakes. I loaded the refurbished printer and watched as it kicked into action. *Whir. Click. Clunk.* The paper disappeared from the tray and into the machine. My anticipation was yearning for the thing to hurry up. Then slowly, line by line, it emerged from the other side. Dorian's impressive physique towering in black-and-white against a corrugated background. The picture was taken by Gary Phillips and watching that iconic image emerge I felt like I was delivering a baby, such was the intensity of effort that had gone into it—physically and emotionally.

I lifted the single piece of paper and felt pride and humility overwhelming me. The warmth of the newly-printed paper and the faint smell of ink in the air are fixed in my memory forever. Here, in a single page, was an expression of my career up until this point. My friends and colleagues had come together to help me produce this premier issue. Without a shadow of doubt, I knew that the late nights and hard work had paid off.

It was a rudimentary affair and to complete the magazine we simply folded it over and used an industrial stapler to fix it together. It could have been a school newspaper for the quality of publication, but I didn't care. It was the content that mattered to me and every word in that magazine was of the highest calibre. And despite the DIY approach, it was aesthetically pleasing to look at.

The pictures were laid out with care and Marika had done a fantastic job of giving them an identity through the design. To the casual reader it might have looked rough and ready but to me it was perfect. From scratch—just a glimmer of an idea less than two months earlier, I had pulled together a full magazine of content that provided the reader with a rich insight into the real world of bodybuilding. This world was the one that I adored, the one that I wanted to share.

With copy number one in my hands, I considered my next step. I'd poured so much energy into making it happen that I hadn't really given a whole heap of thought to marketing and distribution. It was as much as I had ever hoped to have the finished article.

I began cold-calling gyms and independent local newsagents in the hope of getting them to stock *Kaged Muscle*. Surprisingly, quite a few were happy to help me out when I explained the names that were involved and the aim of the magazine. There was something raw and grimy about the issue that appealed to those who shared our passion for bodybuilding.

It was a small start but the feeling of seeing it on the shelf, alongside *FLEX*, *Muscle and Fitness* and the other big names was incredible. Of course, I didn't make any money but the praise came flooding in from fellow athletes and fans alike. We had hit a nerve with our content and the reaction was exhilarating.

Off the back of that initial success, a number of supplement companies approached us to have adverts included, a vital step if we were going to keep it going beyond the first issue. And more athletes jumped on board to get involved in the next one. No sooner had the first hit the shelves that my mind was alive with ideas of how to improve it and add more content. I realised that above everything it was the freedom and control to express things how I really saw it, that drew me to *Kaged Muscle*.

All of this happened alongside my existing commitments to *FLEX* and other magazines that I contributed to. Far from being bitter about my start up, many of the writers offered advice and support seeing the value in what we were bringing to the market. It wasn't competition in any real sense; it was an expression of the hardcore of bodybuilding that tapped into the root of why so many of us were involved in the first place.

Then came the second issue and a third, with features from more giants of the industry. Images from Robert Nailon in Australia, interviews and stories with Flex, Gary Strydom and Marcus Haley. With each iteration we grew in our variety and maturity. Each was tougher than the last but equally rewarding to hold in my hands. Soon, I recruited creative help to make it more professional and while it remained a hobby it was one I both enjoyed and took very seriously.

I would go to Gold's Gym to drop off a dozen issues and come back the next day to discover they'd all gone: the ultimate recognition of work well done. A small drop in the ocean ultimately, but a tidal wave of reward for somebody who just wanted to spread his love for bodybuilding and share the emotion with the world of incredible athletes and champions of the sport. It was the magazine that I'd have wanted as a teenager—filled with my heroes.

11

Moment of Reckoning

Kaged Muscle was a project that emerged from my passion for bodybuilding. I never intended for it to lead anywhere, although I did invest a huge amount of energy into it. It was a side project, a hobby to help me overcome my frustration with conventional publications. In truth, it was always too niche to break beyond the realm of athletes and the hardcore fans.

I did learn an enormous amount during the process. I was no longer simply contributing articles, writing features and taking photographs. I had to consider an entire publication from the front cover to the barcode and from the advertising to the distribution. I had to see the entire picture.

It was a welcome break from what I was uncomfortable with in the articles I was writing for *FLEX*. I was in charge of the editing so I could take the articles where they needed to go, rather than having my messages warped in the re-drafting process. I'm sure the editors had their reasons, I just didn't agree with them a lot of the time.

Around the time of the third issue of *Kaged Muscle* I was attending an event when I met a man by the name of Russ De Luca. He worked with an online publication called *Bodybuilding. com*, for which his son Ryan was the CEO.

were complimenting me with the invite and frankly, I welcomed the opportunity to explore another part of the States.

A few weeks later, I was stepping off a plane that had taken me north to Boise. I was immediately struck by the place. Even driving in from the airport you could see the luscious landscape all around. The city was large but had the uncanny feeling of being small and welcoming at the same time, as though it was the world's biggest town.

Despite being so built up, the city was full of trees and green spaces. Everything about the place was warm and inviting—there was a sense of life and activity everywhere and as we pulled passed parks and rivers there calmness engulfed us. Whereas in Los Angeles, the energy and number of people is almost oppressive and certainly impossible to escape, Boise had this idyllic mixture of space and things going on.

My welcome to Bodybuilding.com was altogether more underwhelming. I approached the address and looked up at what was essentially an enormous warehouse. It was impressive in scale but otherwise fairly nondescript. Tagged onto the other end of the warehouse was a small unassuming office. I knew that Bodybuilding.com got a lot of its revenues from selling supplements (after all, its content was free) so I realised that this must be the reason. I was surprised at just how big it was, far from the operation of the up and coming start-up I presumed it was, they must have been shifting a lot of products to warrant something of that size. And to look inside, you could see an incredible amount of stock from floor to ceiling, of every brand imaginable.

When I entered the office though, I was again brought down to earth. It was a very ordinary-looking old office, the sort I never imagined I would ever work in and it felt very small compared to *FLEX* and other publications I had visited.

These were still early days for Bodybuilding.com. It employed around thirty-five people—across the business—who were responsible for everything: from running the website to posting out the products. The attitude in there was all hands on deck: everyone getting stuck into whatever needed doing. That's something you can't help but love about a small company, there's often an 'all-in-this-together' attitude where you all do what you have to, to make it happen.

I wasn't putting my feet under the table quite yet, as I still knew I had a good job freelancing with *FLEX* and others and I was also enjoying my newly-launched project with *Kaged Muscle*. It would take more than a great city and a good little office atmosphere to win me over and drag me half way across the country. And of course, I would be taking Marika with me as well if I moved so I had gone without any real expectations that Bodybuilding.com could seriously pull us away from Venice.

The big test was the interview with Ryan. Ryan is a pretty private guy so I hadn't met him properly until this point (just a brief encounter at an event) and I had no idea what to expect. We met for lunch at a place called the Olive Garden where we had a light meal and got down to business.

I was struck by how wise, quick witted and sure of himself he seemed, despite the fact he looked and was only twenty-seven. Ryan had set up the business when he was twenty-one. That was an age where I was still riding motocross and hadn't even started working out in the gym. I had no idea where I wanted to go and what I wanted to do with my life and Ryan was building a business from the ground up.

By now, *Bodybuilding.com* had established itself as one of the premier online publications but as I've previously mentioned, bodybuilding was largely confined to magazines. It was playing catch up with the Internet. Except for Ryan. He wasn't playing catch up, he was leading the show.

In a way then, it shouldn't have been surprising how much older Ryan seemed. He'd been doing this for seven years now and he knew the business and the industry very well. He could field any question I had—about where the business was going or how he thought it would change—without a second thought.

When he asked me about bodybuilding, I was equally well qualified and confident. I knew the sport inside out and during my time in Venice I had built up a portfolio of friends and colleagues to rival any writer. I knew the stars old and new, in fact I'd trained with most of them!

But when he asked me where I wanted to take my career he caught me off guard. It sounds a pretty simple interview question but bear in mind that I'd never really gone into any job with a view to where it might lead me. I'd always followed my nose. I had wanted to get out of the UK, so I got on a boat. I enjoyed bodybuilding and the gym so I helped others with their fitness.

Every step I'd taken had been consequential, following a dream that I couldn't quite place my finger on. So when Ryan asked me questions about my future I drew a bit of a blank. I could answer his other questions easily and with confidence, but those few about the long-term threw me and I realised that I needed to start thinking exactly where I wanted to end up.

Ryan talked to me about the mission of Bodybuilding. com. That was something I'd never spent sleepless nights over. There are so many businesses out there that have a single goal: make money. And that's what had frustrated me in Venice—the bigger picture often got lost.

I had come into bodybuilding because of what it gave me and those around me. Control, physically and mentally, to transform myself and my life. It was an incredible feeling to overcome a challenge through the power of transformation.

It was even more humbling to do it for other people. And when you could reach and touch hundreds of thousands of others, that was nirvana.

Somewhere in the glamour of Venice and California I would often lose myself. The showmanship and the vanity that pervaded the industry overshadowed why we were really there. *Kaged Muscle* was born out of my reaction to it all.

Bodybuilding.com shared my belief. The website was run to create a place where the content was free—content was king. Information that would normally come with a cost was given out free of charge to interested people because that's what mattered to Ryan and the Bodybuilding.com team; they wanted as many people as possible to call their website home. The aim was to bring people to visit their website and give them everything that they needed or were looking for.

If the online visitors chose to buy supplements and products through the website, that meant an added bonus. Those did keep the machine rolling for everyone else. For the thousands that didn't, it was enough that the website was spreading the right words. Not the ones pushed by supplement brands or editors to promote a hidden agenda; only good, clean advice for people trying to look after themselves and create a better body and life.

At the end of the interview, Ryan offered me the job there and then. A guy who had barely been writing for a handful of years was being offered the chance to be the Editor-in-Chief for a website that was pumping out dozens of articles a week. He clearly had the gumption to hire somebody like me and that's what completely won me over.

His father, Russ, showed me around Boise. My first impressions had been brilliant. But these following impressions after the interview were even better. I hadn't for even a second imagined that a relatively backwater city in the States could blow me away but everything about the place felt right.

As for Bodybuilding.com, my mind was racing with the potential the company had. And the things that it stood for. Ryan had these huge plans and I wanted to be part of them.

I phoned Marika to talk to her about how the interview had gone. Initially, I teased her it had been a waste of a trip but then I told her the truth: that I wanted us to move there and I was overjoyed at the opportunity. Ryan had sold me the idea and the place was a dream come true.

Marika was as surprised at this change of heart, but she backed me all the way. Within a matter of weeks we were relocating all of our possessions to our new apartment in Boise. I was throwing myself fully at this new challenge, one that I can only describe as feeling right; like the moment you find the final piece of a jigsaw that fits perfectly.

I wasn't naïve to think that what I was taking on wasn't an enormous challenge. For the first time in my career, I felt daunted by what I was up against. My experience of running a publication from the bottom up was no more than a handful of *Kaged Muscle* magazines. And whereas there I had been calling upon friends to contribute a couple of stories here and there over a few months, this was on an entirely different scale.

As I've said, Bodybuilding.com was a relatively small operation at the time but it was still responsible for creating as much as forty different articles a week. That was more than I was used to being responsible for in a year with all of my writing. Of course, I wouldn't be writing all of them but they would be my responsibility and that responsibility was some weight.

The second, and perhaps biggest, challenge in my eyes was the fact that virtually all of the content that we were creating was by writers who weren't paid for their work. How could we ensure the quantity and quality of writing required when ultimately people were doing it out of their love for the industry? How could you push and cajole people into pulling their finger out to hit a deadline when they were already doing a day job?

For Ryan, these were questions he faced every day and came up trumps. For me, they were new and quite frightening, at least initially.

The third challenge was a practical one. Here I was in charge of dozens of pieces of content on a website when I barely knew how to use a computer—never mind update a website. For the first few months, I lived in almost constant fear that I would press a button and accidentally delete Bodybuilding. com. In reality, that was never possible, but it was certainly true that you could end up deleting or damaging the code for an entire page if you didn't know what you were doing.

I was the dinosaur of the office. My bulky frame huddled over the keyboard prodding each letter with my index fingers one by one. I had used computers before but I'd never had to rely upon them like this. *Click, click, click.* A long pause while I worked out how to create a new paragraph in the coding I had been given. And then click. *Click. Click.*

It was a laborious process using only two fingers and for the guys who had grown up with a keyboard as an extension of their hands it must have been painful to watch. Fortunately, Ryan had a guy called Will look after me initially to help me get up and going and make sure the caveman of the Internet 2.0 didn't crash the site.

They also provided me with some games that I could play at home. These games helped develop the dexterity I needed to control the computer with more than two fingers and over time I became, if not adept, at least proficient in the basics. That was important because it freed me up to do the things I was actually good at.

At the time, Bodybuilding.com was at an important juncture. The Internet was changing from one that was static and one way—i.e. people clicked on a link and read an article, maybe with a couple of pictures. This was a versatile and multi-faceted world where people could interact with content, each other and the website itself.

Ryan and Bodybuilding.com were riding a wave of change. In fact, for our industry, they weren't just riding the wave, they were creating it. In 2006 Ryan had launched Bodyspace—a forum in which Bodybuilding.com users could meet and share ideas and information, support one another in goals and build a community for fitness and health enthusiasts.

Dozens of others were trying to do the same, off the back of the success stories of MySpace and then Facebook. It was the dawn of social media as we would once understand and all sorts of industries were trying it from retail to sport; entertainment to fashion. It was the in-thing to try and emulate the success of those start-ups and create your own thriving community.

What Ryan had recognised though, was that our industry was fertile ground for this sort of community. It wasn't a token effort, it was perfectly suited to people who were passionate about health and fitness and were evangelical about its impact. It had needed something like this for decades and now that the technology was there, Bodyspace was simply filling a gap.

The numbers reflected this and by the time I had arrived, there were 100,000 users and that number would surge to 1,000,000 by 2011. It was an active and vibrant community of people that gathered to support the cause. I encouraged everybody from the recreational bodybuilder to the hardcore of bodybuilders to use the forum. This kind of an engagement allowed everyone to find like-minded aspirants and feel motivated and confident.

Bodyspace is just one example of the kind of change that was happening when I joined. Multimedia content was also surging ahead. Videos, interactive content and transformation plans, live webcasts—these were things that the industry could only have dreamed of previously.

For somebody in Wales whose only access to Mr. Olympia had been through the pages of magazines ten years ago, could now enjoy the wonders of live streaming of the event without any hiccups or unnecessary delays. Bodybuilding.com brought the excitement and energy right into the homes. Not just Wales but every corner of the world: from Mumbai to Moscow and Tokyo to Tanzania, Bodybuilding.com (and a handful of competitors, I should add) were making the sport global and accessible for the first time. And the most incredible part of it, they were doing it for free.

For me, Bodybuilding.com required a change in terms of mindset and writing style. I was used to writing for an audience that was interested in bodybuilding in the very narrow sense of the sport. Bodybuilding.com was centred on that sport but reached out to everyone from new mums to people with eating disorders. It pitched itself perfectly as an expert on everything and that meant my writing needed to be more encompassing than I was affording through *Kaged Muscle* or even my articles for *FLEX*.

This presented another challenge before me and I was up for it. I had to read far more widely on a range of subjects and sports than I had previously, in order, to educate myself on the variety of content we were publishing. I had to be as comfortable with plyometrics as with massaging. Some of it was entirely new; some simply required me dusting off brain cells from my earlier career. But I thrived upon all of it. I was learning more than I had ever before and getting paid for it.

My early days at Bodybuilding.com were largely about building up a bit of momentum and knowledge of how everything worked. I was also getting to grips with my new location, which I had fallen head over heels in love with. Boise was a perfect blend of everything I had searched for in Australia and California: alive with energy when you wanted it, secluded and private when you didn't.

The range of sports and outdoor activities was phenomenal. I was able to pick up downhill mountain biking again (I had done a bit back in Wales) and snowboarding. Situated in the foothills of the Rockies, Boise is surrounded by green forests, towering mountains, lakes and rivers. Nature was never more than a short drive away and even in the city I never really nursed the idea of escape.

After a few months of living in an apartment next to the river, Marika and I started looking for a home. The word 'home' is important because it says a lot about how my mindset had changed. I wanted to find more than a place to live and work, I wanted a place to call home. It was no longer enough to simply rent a place that could service my lifestyle I was so content with; I needed to begin building something more permanent.

Marika and I must have been to thirty different houses in search of something. There was never a goldilocks 'just right' place though. All of them seemed to have a drawback of some sort. Part of the problem was that our values were quite different to those of Americans. In the States, a huge amount of value is placed around how old a property is. The very fact that a building was made in 1930 lends it with more heritage than half the country. For me from Wales and Marika from Sweden, where there are thousands of houses that are older than The

White House, it was hardly important whether the house was new or fifty years old.

We wanted a blank canvas—somewhere that we could make into a home. After dozens of failed attempts we finally came across something that fitted the bill. It was a house that had been left nearly-finished after the builders had gone bankrupt. Perhaps the fact it needed some work would put most people off, but I saw potential. It had a distinctly European feel, which was important to both of us, and the garden and much of the house were devoid of anybody else's influence. It was ours to make into a home.

I had a friend called Nick Holt, acting as our estate agent, looking after the negotiations. He was fantastic and kept all the plates spinning whilst I got on with the day job at Bodybuilding. com. That was vital because we were due to be closing on the place right in the middle of the Arnold Classic, which was hardly conducive to my schedule.

In order that we could make it happen, Nick, also a fan of bodybuilding flew out to Columbus with me. I was neck deep in work and barely had a moment's rest between the various jobs I had to undertake on behalf of Bodybuilding.com. This was a long stretch from the days where I'd turned up for *FLEX Australia*, done some cursory work before enjoying the event as a fan. I was dashing from booth to show to exposition hall to backstage interviewing, organising and reporting.

During those brief moments that I could stop and breathe, Nick would grab me to sign a piece of paperwork which would then be faxed off. It was manic but by the time I sat down to catch my breath at the end of the weekend, I was the proud owner of the house I intended to make a home.

When I say it was a blank canvas, I'm not exaggerating. The garden was nothing more than a field of mud. I was starting from scratch. With the help of another friend called Jim Britain, I designed and set about making a Japanese Garden—of the sort that is usually reserved for a botanical garden. I wanted to capture the distinctive tranquillity that can only be felt when wandering between cherry blossoms, pebble-fringed pools of water and low drooping trees. It took months to build and a heck of a lot of maintenance, but once it was complete I had my own piece of paradise.

What had clinched the sale for me was the bathroom. The bedroom was separated from it by a piece of glass that could be obscured or left transparent, opening up the bathroom with its enormous claw foot bath sitting imperiously in full view.

Safe in the knowledge that I intended to be here for a long time, I set about decorating the place to the last detail. Never being one for hanging pictures from the wall, I imported large transfers from Europe that could be applied to the walls imitating telegraph poles, bubbles, flowers and coat hangers. I purchased a fish tank that hung flat from the wall creating an underwater world in my living room.

I bought a black-and-white sofa for the living room that—while not being the most comfortable to sit on—created a huge space for friends who would come and watch Ultimate Fighting Championship on the gigantic screen.

It was my own world, my creation. A home built from my imagination over the course of months and then years that provided a colourful and comfortable backdrop for my work at Bodybuilding.com.

Work itself was ramping up. I was travelling more and more as I jetted off to cover events, interview athletes and attend meetings. The website was on an exponential upwards curve as it drew in ever increasing traffic and support from the industry.

The level of coverage we were able to, and wanted to, offer was on a dramatic rise as well. Whereas previously we might have done a couple of interviews with athletes in the week leading up to Mr. Olympia or the Arnold Classic, we were now meeting up with competitors ten weeks ahead of the event to film them in training and build up a huge hoard of content that would leave our audience's appetite whetted for the main event.

The atmosphere in the office was changing quickly, too. From that little room of people I'd met before my interview, there were new faces every single day or so it felt like. Such was the growth that we moved to a new location and a new warehouse. I would queue up for food in the canteen, turn around and see this wall of young new staff full of energy—I could barely keep up and I never even began to learn everyone's names.

The place had a unique character that people either fitted into or didn't. It took a special kind of person to keep up with the pace but those who could and quickly became part of the furniture. They lived and breathed the Bodybuilding.com mission and would work until they dropped to hit a deadline.

I was now working with the most motivated and talented workforce I had ever come into contact with. I was leading many of them, in our budding talented set of writers and contributors. The mindset we adopted in the lead up to our busiest times of the year, like January, where we would need to collate enormous swathes of content, was one of a single collective unit. Our band of brothers would rally together to overcome ever increasing hurdles as they flew at us faster and faster.

Personally, I was challenged by Ryan to pick up a gauntlet that I was avoiding, of becoming a public face and taking advantage of my only recognisable image in the industry. This started with the Daily Video Trainer. Normally, I would prefer to be the one behind the camera lens, directing and organising—but with this video series I would be the focus of attention.

It was part of Ryan's big plan. That Bodybuilding.com should have its own expert trainer—and for free. There are dozens of videos out there to help people with a transformation or fitness regime but they do so in one or two or three instalments. Just enough to fill a DVD but not enough to maintain your motivation on a day to day basis like a personal trainer can.

The idea behind the Daily Video Trainer is exactly as it sounds—to give you a daily snapshot of motivation and the ability to track your progress against mine. Initially, I wasn't keen on the idea of being the centre of attention, but it came together just so perfectly that I couldn't say no.

It all started several months earlier when I had been doing some downhill mountain biking in the foothills. I'd gotten seriously into the sport since I'd arrived in Boise and it took me back to my teenage years when I would try it only to give my motocross a rest.

My problem back then was that I would try and race as though I was on a motorbike flying down the hill at breakneck speed before losing control and flying into a tree. In Boise, I was able to get the hang of it a little more sensibly but I was still tearing through the woods, relishing the adrenaline rush as the wind whistled around me and I ducked under branches and bounced from tree stump to tree stump.

One day, I was attacking a particularly tough downhill section, nipping from side to side as quickly as my frame would allow me when I felt my brakes go. My heart leapt out of my chest as I saw a drop approaching and I realised I wouldn't be able to slow down. The next thing I knew I was being shaken awake by Marika. My head was throbbing and I could barely work out which part of me hurt the most as pain ebbed from elbows to knees to hands. Marika drifted in and out of focus as I tried to rebuild what had happened, vaguely remembering the sight of the handlebars disappearing beneath me as I was hurled forward.

To begin with, I couldn't move my upper body which scared the hell out of me. For a moment, I thought I might have suffered a back injury resulting in part paralysis, the kind of thing that can not only end a sporting career but leave you with disabilities for life. Slowly, once the adrenalin had begun to wear off and pain stung like bullets through my body, I was able to get up cautiously and with Marika's support.

I hobbled back to the car, covered in cuts and growing bruises. There was a telltale discomfort in my back that I hadn't felt since my motocross days and I could barely close my fists without sharp shots of pain firing up my wrists. After a couple of hours at home trying to pretend it might clear up on its own, I sought medical advice and after an MRI scan was told that in the course of coming off the bike I'd torn my pectoral minor as well as some tendon, but most worryingly, the AC joints in my shoulder had got separated. I also had a black eye and ear and a grazed face, but I knew from experience that these things healed. The bigger concern was whether there might be lasting damage.

The net result was that I was out of most of my weight training for a month. For somebody who lived and died by the gym, looking after their body, this was the worst thing that could have happened to me. I was devastated. I was able to do some light leg work but it took a very long time to train up my upper body again and some exercises like barbell bench presses would be beyond me for good.

It took a month of religious rehabilitation of my shoulder joint to repair the damage, during which time I put on a significant amount of weight for the first time in many years. I was out of shape and I needed something to get me back to my peak.

The Daily Video Trainer was in effect then a personal diary of my return from the abyss. It tracked me as I attempted to transform myself from 230 pounds to a competition weight of 190 pounds in just three months. It followed not only this physical transformation but also a mental one as I overcame injury and the anxiety of the journey from being out of action through to my return to my former level of fitness.

As always, I needed something to work toward: a goal that would make me accountable at the end of the three months, and would also ensure I remained motivated for the duration of the filming taking place at my house every day.

This meant a return to competition after the frustration of the World Championships: the bittersweet experience of being on the world stage but being consigned to the now soul-destroying position of runner up.

It was an enormous step for me to make but one which Ryan encouraged me to take. I had demons to put to bed and the way everything had come together, with the injury and the video trainer series, made this the right time for me to get back on the horse.

The competition I would be taking part in was no slouch—it was a different federation to the one I had previously entered and was for the State of Idaho. This was the first time I would be competing on US soil, where natural bodybuilding was huge, and I would be up against more than 100 other bodybuilders. The icing on the cake was that it would be held in Boise and so, for the first time, I would also be competing in front of a home crowd—the pressure was on.

During the lead up to the competition, a friend from Wales came to live with me for a while. The friend was a guy called

Chopper, who had in fact been the lead singer of the band I was good friends with in Builth Wells. It was the very same Chopper who had held me back when I pinned the drummer for sleeping with my girlfriend, Suzie. We had stayed in touch and he had come over to snowboard and was staying with me.

Chopper had never done any bodybuilding while we were back in Wales but the guy was naturally quite lean and he decided to give it a go while he was with me. He was great to have around and although he was only entering the first-timers category, there was no direct competition. On the contrary, it was useful to have somebody else in the same mindset as me.

Because he was so lean, Chopper needed virtually no preparation time and actually only started dieting three weeks down before we were due on stage. For most people, this would mean suicide as you would never get the fat off in time, but for Chopper it was almost too long. He was harbouring barely a handful of per cent of body fat by the big day and I believe he would have probably killed himself if he had carried on much longer. I, on the other hand, had been working a solid twelve weeks out and, cometh the moment I was as pumped and lean as ever.

The venue for the competition was a matter of minutes away from my house. On the day I travelled down to take part in the pre-screening where polygraph tests were being carried out. The experience is always odd because while of course you know you've done nothing wrong, you're hooked up to this machine and being asked all kinds of questions from what you've got in your garage through to how many pets you have. Then amongst all of the small talk they suddenly interrogate you as to whether you have taken testosterone.

Having got through that and the other formalities, I headed home. That was the advantage to being so close. While I had the added nerves of facing my friends in the crowd, I was so nearby that I could get away from all the tension and the build up and head to my house where I could clear my mind of it all and focus. In previous events, I had been forced to hang around and watch as competitors readied up and flexed their muscles. Inevitably, this had always made me nervous and I'm sure that was apparent on stage.

After Toronto, I couldn't face those nerves anymore. That feeling of horrible anxiety as the fear of second place weighed over me like the grim reaper taunting me with the prospect of humiliation. I knew that Ryan, Chopper and the others would be proud of me whatever I did on stage but for me this ran deep now. It was the most fiercely competitive Idaho State Championship in history and I was determined that I wouldn't let myself down. The road back from injury had been a dark one and now I had finally come back to the stage after three years of being out of the limelight, I had to avoid those last-minute nerves as much as possible.

I had asked a friend to keep me up to date with the time I would be called on for the finals and as it approached I was still at home, mentally preparing but in the safety of my own four walls. I got the call to say we were on in thirty minutes and I began the final warm-ups that could be the difference between success and failure.

By now, my posing routine was second nature. I flew through it and felt a glow of pride that I had made it back onto the stage after everything I had been through. The path from Toronto to Boise had twisted and turned my life in a number of directions, but here I was facing the same challenge I had five times previously.

On stage I could barely stand, the knot in my chest tightening and the nausea overwhelming me. When I had done my routine, the crowd had been alive, roaring me on and full of friendly faces that I had tried desperately to tune out.

Now, there was pin drop silence and the tension was at breaking point. My friends couldn't know what the moment meant to me but they had a reasonable idea. The hushed tone filled the air as the anticipation of the decisive moment approached like a ghost train pulling into a station inch by inch.

The MC cleared his throat and began to read out the names. The pauses between each contestant seemed to hang on for minutes on end and I'm not sure that I remembered to breathe the entire time. My heart was racing and I was begging for redemption and relief.

Fourth place came and went as always. Then, third. Then, it was the turn of my nemesis: "Second place..." An achingly long pause was broken by somebody else's name.

I could barely believe it. My groundhog day had been broken.

"First place: Kris Gethin."

My heart was racing and I felt the blood rush to my head as the moment sunk in. My curse finally lifted, I felt as though I could finally stand up straight; a weight that had been my burden for nearly ten years was removed.

I can hardly remember the moments that followed because I was physically and emotionally drained by the entire experience. It was the culmination of another twelve weeks of transformation that had given me the purpose I needed so badly after the pain of my back injury.

I wasn't the only one celebrating victory that day. Quite incredibly, given his short lead up, Chopper had claimed the title in his first-timer event. Together with Marika and my Bodybuilding.com family we went to a local pancake house to commemorate the occasion and hog on delicious food.

I ate until my stomach hurt and collapsed in a happy haze of relief. Chopper, not used to being so utterly emaciated couldn't stop eating. He just kept going and going—to look at him you couldn't understand how he was doing it.

The next day when we woke up, I felt a new sense of purpose. The clouds that had been gathering around me cleared and I felt inspired to continue on the path I had carved out in Boise. Chopper, in contrast, could barely walk. From almost starving himself to death he was now walking around like some cartoon character bloated like a balloon from the sheer quantity of food and fluid he had taken on board.

The whole experience from crashing off the bike in the woods to standing on stage and hearing those vital words was life affirming. I knew that the moment was a defining one and after talking to Ryan I made sure I would never attempt to do so. I commissioned a series of tattoos that would cover my back so extensively that I would never seriously be able to enter a bodybuilding competition again. Those tattoos were not outlets of relief, like my piercings and tattoos previously. They were a badge of honour that I had overcome my personal demons—something that could never be taken away. They made that moment on stage in Boise permanent and everlasting.

12

Failing to Succeed

It feels a bit strange to look back at the period that followed my success on stage. Things were going from strength to strength and with the release that victory gave me, I felt free to take more risks and explore further opportunities.

I had already delved into a spot of auto trading, following in my father's footsteps of entrepreneurialism. I would buy up VW Beetles from Idaho and Arizona and take them to the coast. Because it was drier in Arizona and Idaho, they would often be in much better condition than an equivalent model in say Seattle, where the wet weather would corrode the body over time.

As a result, the driveway was always jammed with Campers and Beetles that I was buying and selling. This drove Marika up the wall because they would spill oil and stink out the house. It was a good earner though and from my days back in Wales where I had owned one I knew my way around the vehicle when it came to fixing odds and ends—which is often all you need to bump up the value.

There was never any serious risk attached to what I was doing, so I decided to look at other ways of making the money I was earning in the day job. The obvious step was to look into property development, especially given my father's success doing the same in Wales. I wasn't worried that I might suffer the same problem as in Australia and the place in Hunter's Valley because I was so absolutely certain that this was where I wanted to be. I couldn't imagine leaving.

With some help and advice from friends, I decided to invest the savings I had accrued into buying a set of flats in a place called Nampa, also in Idaho. The city wasn't as quaint as Boise but it was growing fast, tripling in size over just 20 years. It seemed a solid bet that they would hold their value given the rapidity at which the place was growing. They did need quite a bit of work but I was able to land a deal following a lot of negotiation tactics I had learned from my father. I loved the challenge of getting them up to scratch.

Over the course of a few months we put the two flats back together again. The plan was that I would rent them back out which would chip away at the debt I'd taken on to buy them. I felt good that I had been able to invest my time and energy into something so worthwhile, though I didn't plan to use them myself. The place was rented out easily and I got on with other projects.

One of my closest friends at Bodybuilding.com was a guy called Brandon Poe who worked in the video department. We would spend a lot of time together outside of work, working out in the gym, camping or just hanging out. He also competed in bodybuilding contests, albeit in the lightweight categories, so we were as thick as thieves.

One weekend that year, I managed to sell one of the VW Beetles and received a motocross bike for free as part of the deal. Brandon and I decided to take it out for a spin, with him on a 250cc bike and me on this much smaller 125cc one. I was back in my element, although it had been more than ten years since I had last sat on a bike, and it didn't matter that he had the bigger engine—I was flying around with all the daring and recklessness of my early 20s. It was a real rush to be pushing those limits again.

When I got off the bike I knew I could never get back on though. For all the thrill, I knew I wouldn't be satisfied biking unless I was hammering it. I couldn't hold back because that was the only way I knew how to ride. But I wasn't in my early 20s anymore and my body didn't repair itself in the same way.

If I took a serious fall, I could end up back at square one with my fitness (which was my livelihood) or worse. I'd been shaken up by my mountain bike fall and those few seconds where I couldn't move my upper body. I had to see things in perspective and get my endorphins from something that I didn't need to push quite so close to the edge to enjoy.

At Bodybuilding.com, I experienced a slow shift in and realignment of roles over time. The success of the video series confirmed my position as an increasingly useful spokesperson for the company. I was becoming the face and name associated with the brand, which suited Ryan. He was running the show in the background but he didn't want the publicity, his reward was the success of the website and in particular, the incredible stories that were coming out of Bodyspace as people embarked on transformations.

It didn't happen overnight but very quickly the video series gathered pace and popularity. The stories on Bodyspace started to trickle and then flood through; we saw more and more people who had completely changed their lives because they had found support and advice in the daily trainer. The immense weight of pride and responsibility dawned on me reading through their stories. There were people who had come close to suicide because their lives had spiralled out of control. Taking charge of their bodies had given them a new hope, a new way to lift their anxieties and to transform physically and mentally.

I'd always known on a personal level how important bodybuilding and fitness were to my own happiness and sense of control. To see the thousands of others going through the same experience was humbling.

I began to understand that when I let my standards slip it was no longer just myself that I let down. I remember one episode when I was inside the theatre and a friend went to pass me some popcorn. At the last minute I remembered to decline, recalling that a few rows back there was somebody who had recognised me and had thanked me for the inspiration I had been.

I wasn't vain enough to believe that I should put myself on a pedestal to be admired—I just realised that my actions were now accountable to a greater audience. If I couldn't hold up my end of the bargain, how could those following my programme would? I might not have had my competitions to work toward as goals, but in a way I had something stronger within. The accountability was always there and it didn't stop after twelve weeks—it was constant.

No sooner had the success of the daily trainer began to sink in than I was already working on another project. This time I was to write a book, designed to help people to get the body they wanted by fostering the right motivation. It stemmed from what we had seen first-hand on Bodyspace, dozens of people supporting one another in their aims and being greatly more successful as a result.

The idea is quite simple really but too often ignored. If you could surround yourself with people who wanted to join you on your push to take control of your life, you would have a network that could support, advise and most importantly hold you accountable to your goals. The reality to find these people isn't always easy. Your family and friends might be living the very lifestyle you're trying to escape.

Bodyspace was tapping into this problem, by grouping people together to guarantee that accountability. Because if you've said out loud to somebody that you're going to commit to go to the gym, to eat healthy and to stick it out the long run—you are far more likely to do so. There's no shying away from thinking, "Well, I'm only letting myself down".

It's also powerful to be spending time and energy in an environment that encourages and reinforces good talks and discussions on fitness and health. Imagine you were living in a world where everybody else had sixty per cent body fat and you only had forty per cent body fat. So when you look around, you say to yourself, "Hey, I'm in pretty good shape". Nobody in that world cares about fitness, they don't talk about it nor do they ever think about what is in their food. So you don't either, because we normalise our lives against those around us.

This is the reality for millions around the world today and it is getting worse. In the pockets of low-income communities in developed countries, the mentality about taking care of health and body is changing. The only way to break this is to wake up and surround yourself with people who share your attitude and give you realistic perspective about your body.

I should add that the most powerful thing about Bodyspace is that it doesn't simply attract people looking to lose weight. Certainly, that's the most common health issue facing us, but Bodyspace is about more than shedding the pounds. It's about getting the body that is right for you. And there are countless cases of people with eating disorders such as anorexia, who have been able to overcome them through taking control during a transformation. Equally, there are people who have lost limbs but are challenging their perceived disability.

That was the foundation of my first book, *Body by Design*. We wanted to provide people, regardless of their background or circumstance, with the ability to take control of their life and their body.

Working on the manuscript was quite different to what I had been doing up until this point. I was out of the office, sitting in coffee shops. I was researching and gathering stories of inspiration and gradually building them into a coherent guide. There was a diet and a workout plan but all this came after the motivation which was instilled in the same way as Bodyspace, by telling the stories of others who had beaten off excuses to transform themselves. Whatever your personal fitness roadblocks, you should be able to look and see somebody else who has already overcome them.

Writing a book isn't like thrashing out an article for a magazine and it required a huge amount of patience and diligence to make it a reality. With the help of our literary agent, we secured the interest and support of our publisher. And while initially we were selling the idea to them, like so many others in Bodyspace, we watched them grow to believe in it as much as we did it.

Finally, landing the deal followed a memorable few days running from meeting to meeting in a foot of snow in New York. It was a fantastic new experience meeting ten plus of the world's biggest publication houses over three days and telling them about my book. Stephen had years of experience under his belt at several of these houses and as an agent he was brilliant—and a lot of fun.

When you're gaining momentum, as I was (and Bodybuilding.com was), you barely have time to stop and doubt yourself. The power of belief breeds itself and I was very swiftly building up a head of steam off the back of my bodybuilding finale. The book was coming together perfectly well. After the daily trainer, it made sense and it didn't matter that it was merely months since we had launched it, we had to strike while the iron was hot.

It also gave me an enormous amount of self confidence. I began to explore my own ideas, fuelled by my desire to push the limits of my ability and capacity. I didn't want to sit still.

With all of the travelling, flying in and out of cities, I was finding it increasingly difficult to maintain my diet. I always managed but it wasn't simple. I hadn't missed a meal in approaching a decade by this point and I began to wonder whether, if the products weren't out there to give me what I needed, I could make them myself.

Brandon from Bodybuilding.com had a friend who he thought might be able to help. The guy, Ruben Navaratte, was introduced to me as someone who ran a business that helped people get ideas about launching companies. From creating surfboards to computer components—he worked out the logistics for me and guided me well.

I explained the challenge I faced and the idea I had to overcome it. The problem for bodybuilders like me, or even someone just looking to get in shape is that we need, a very strict, regular and specific diet to maintain the right amount of nutrition in our bodies. Getting this normally, when you have time and access to a kitchen, can be tough. But doing it while you're on the go or in a rush can be nigh on impossible and is a really common excuse for people giving up their transformations.

There are plenty of snacks out there in the fitness market, protein bars and supplements for instance. But, there are very few meals or probably none that can be carried on the go. If you're flying, in particular, then having to cart around the sheer weight of the fluids in your food becomes a nightmare.

My concept was to introduce a range of nutritious freeze-dried meals without preservatives. There was ample evidence that it could work—after all, there are freeze-dried meals used by everyone from students to NASA! However, all of the ones on the market had extremely poor nutritional value, high in saturated fats and laced with sodium.

Ruben was as excited by the idea as I was and I was so impressed by his passion that I didn't want him to simply help me launch the line as with other clients, I wanted him to be my business partner for the venture. We agreed to go in 50/50 on creating and launching something to fill the gap I'd identified. We called the project Nutrition by Design and embarked on the huge challenge of finding out whether the thing I had described could even be manufactured, starting by testing formulas.

I had lots of plates spinning but I was also enjoying life. I had settled down in Boise and earned a family of friends from Bodybuilding.com to keep me motivated, always. Ryan was an exceptional leader, inspirational boss and a great-natured person.

He instilled a unique working environment and atmosphere in the offices. We were part of a company that was growing so quickly that it was hard to keep up with. Each month the numbers of unique visitors we were getting would spike as rapidly as our workforce was growing. The few dozen people we had set out with when I'd joined were now in the hundreds and showing no sign of slowing down.

It took a very particular type of person to work there and Ryan had to run a ship that kept the right ones there and let those, who didn't fit, go on their way. He made tough decisions that ensured we maintained the momentum integral to any company looking to break the dominance of pre-existing publications.

At the same time, he was one of us. When he could take a moment's breather, and he wasn't with his lovely family, he always made time to see us. He would hold BBQs, or take us to his favourite pancake house or head over the Nevada border to indulge us in a spot of gambling. It kept him fresh and we loved his company, despite the fact he was ultimately our boss.

One of my favourite memories is going to the Sasquatch! Music Festival in Washington State. The festival was set in the Gorge Amphitheatre which is surrounded by huge Grand Canyon-esque rock formations. With this stunning backdrop we were able to watch the likes of Nine Inch Nails and Jane's Addiction—two of the bands I'd grown up listening to in Wales.

There are tonnes of brilliant music festivals in the States, but, perhaps because of the other worldly setting, this was by far and away the one that I enjoyed the most. It was also because I was there with my friends from Bodybuilding.com, including Ryan who, reluctantly, agreed on our second trip there to join us in staying over by bringing along an enormous camper van for us to stay in.

It's a measure of how busy we were at the time that Ryan and I hadn't managed to hold my work evaluation until this point. So in between bands and crowd surfing we found a quiet spot and chatted about how I was getting on and where I wanted to go.

Ryan was brilliant for this. At so many jobs, evaluations are just an excuse for your boss to bust your balls about the mistakes you've made. Ryan wasn't interested in sweating over the past or niggling details. He wanted to talk about how I could build on my strengths and push along the path that I was forging for myself. He would see the employee's success as tied to that of the company, so he had every reason to want them to succeed.

He was also a visionary. The kind where it's hard to even put a finger on what it is that sets them apart—other than the fact that they're always right! There would be plenty of occasions where I would worry that some of our competitors might be copying some of our ideas or riding on our coat-tails, but Ryan would calm me down and tell me to hold our course.

Ryan knew our next steps years before the rest of us—he was planning it out long before the chess pieces moved into position. Time and again the industry was playing catch up with Bodybuilding.com because by the time somebody was competing with one feature or piece of content, we had ten more on the go.

His leadership bred an almost uncongenial atmosphere in office. Perhaps, because he was so charismatic in person, and equally comfortable in the boardroom, wearing a mullet wig and playing Guitar Hero with us, we would have done anything for him.

Every time I got a message or an email from somebody on Bodyspace telling me how I had helped them overcome the darkest days of their life, I knew it was really Ryan who they should be thanking. He was the one who persuaded me to get in front of the camera, and brought people together through his website and company. He was the one who had worked day and night in the earliest and hardest and had never stopped believing in his idea, when others might have fallen by the wayside.

When Stacey called me in to explain the problem with my visa, in the autumn of 2010, it was of course Ryan who I looked to for advice. Unfortunately, despite being wise beyond his years, this was one answer he didn't have.

It was a moment of horror that threatened everything.

13

A Hard Fall: Part II

The team at Bodybuilding.com could have washed its hands of me at that point. There were plenty of people just as capable of fulfilling my role and they owed me nothing. Ryan had given me the opportunity and it wasn't his fault that I was in this position.

After a decade of filing paperwork on time and diligently making sure my visas were in order since leaving the UK in 1999, I had finally slipped. I hadn't been at fault but the person whom I had entrusted with that responsibility had. It was a horror of a situation, unfolding painfully piece by piece.

Soon it became clear that it wasn't going to be a smooth ride. Back in the UK with my parents and having faced that initial rejection I felt trapped. I had everything I wanted in Boise. I was that most precious of things: content. And it had slipped away and left me on the outside looking in.

More or less, immediately I had to step down as Editor-in-Chief for *Bodybuilding.com*. In effect, they had been employing me illegally, so my position was untenable. They didn't abandon me though, far from it. The lawyers poured energy into my case. I was made, initially, a Deputy Editor. In terms of the law, I was being rehired as a contractor. And a guy called Jeff O'Connell took over my position as Editor-in-Chief. I wasn't bitter at all. In a way, I was ecstatic that I wasn't being given my marching orders. Ryan never wavered in his support and kept finding ways for me to be of use from across the ocean.

The work on *Body by Design* was still taking up a lot of my time. And I kept busy writing articles and more than anything, trying to pull together the information I thought I needed for my case. The book in particular was something I felt very guilty about. Although I'd done nothing wrong I knew I was letting Bodybuilding.com and the publishers down in my absence. Less so to begin with whilst we were still writing but as we went on and after publication, I was unable to support its launch with personal bookshop appearances and the top TV shows in the US they had planned for me to feature on.

In terms of my day-to-day work at Bodybuilding.com, the gradual shift that I had been making from being Editor-in-Chief to more of a spokesperson working with the marketing team meant I wasn't completely useless. Admittedly, I couldn't go to events in the US but we had a reasonable presence in Europe and the UK. And after a few months, and the slow and gradual realisation that I wasn't going home any time soon, I became a travelling ambassador for the brand.

The first of these events was a trip to Australia where I held a seminar at the new Titan Fitness gym on Coogee beach in Sydney. The place was owned by the same person (Mets) who had held my 700 pound squat lift photo shoot in his gym days before I left Australia. This new place was hands down the finest gym I have ever seen—from its cleanliness, to equipment, to atmosphere and location. I really enjoyed the sense that I was spreading the word about Bodybuilding.com to new corners of the world. If you believe in what you're selling—it's much easier. I've always been evangelical about Ryan and Bodybuilding.com.

I was also working hard with Ruben on Nutrition by Design, our range of freeze-dried meals. The early stages were frustrating and far more time consuming than I had imagined. The amount of work in even getting food on the shelves caught me off guard.

It had taken us three months to create a formula that would, in theory, work. The major sticking points were the number of foods that just couldn't go together. For instance, a bodybuilder would normally get high amounts of protein from egg white and oats—but the glucose would brown the egg whites in the form we were trying to make them. It was such a fine balancing act.

Eventually, we settled on the creation of a chicken, and a beef with chilli and brown rice dish. Simple meals that would contain the nutrition the body needed. We sent off for a sample to be made up from our recipe and before too long we had our first sample back. The nutritional profile was spot on, with nearly 35g of protein in each cup. But the taste wasn't quite right. So back to the drawing board we went.

It was time consuming but the intensity and level of detail needed allowed me to keep my mind occupied and moving at the hardest points during my exile in Wales. From the moment we came up with the idea to the final product took fifteen months, with a different formula being tested on almost a monthly basis. We would tweak, send it back and still have to wait three to six weeks.

I was frustrated but the end result was worth it. We always knew it was going to be a big task to achieve what we wanted but with grit, determination and some sterling work by Ruben, we got there. In this cycle of trying and re-trying, the costs kept mounting significantly. And the further you got along, the harder it was to turn back. Thankfully, we never gave up.

Give up I could have though because money was becoming a real issue. The houses that I had bought as an investment while I was in Idaho were killing me. The tenants had abandoned the house with the rent in arrears and the place in a sorry state. Around the same time, the housing market was collapsing and I found myself at sea.

The sums weren't adding up and working through them with my father I was becoming increasingly scared as to how I could keep all of the plates spinning whilst being on the wrong side of the world. I couldn't go to the houses and sort them out—I was powerless to stop things unravelling.

When I went to the embassy in London for the second time, I was really at last chance saloon. The rejection I received again didn't kill my chances of returning to the States but it meant that my time had run out. I was devastated and I knew what was coming.

I tried running the numbers every which way but eventually my father told me it was time to let go. I foreclosed on the mortgages for the houses I was letting. And I had to foreclose on the home I had built from the garden upwards at a big loss of thousands of dollars.

My life was falling to pieces and the solutions were always just beyond my grasp. I felt utterly powerless in a way I never had, even as a child.

I felt like I had regressed from standing tall and proud and walking on my own two feet, to a shadow of myself. My parents went to the US for several weeks on my behalf and with the help of my good friend Nick Holt they took all of the things from my house and put them into storage. That was three years ago and those possessions are still gathering dust.

Things had fallen apart at such a speed and with such a series of consistent blows that I began to wonder whether

I would ever recover. Even though my heart was still in that place in Boise, and my life there, I was watching as any possibility of returning to that life slipped away.

As I fought for my visa waiver, it was that life that I was fighting to retain. But if I finally had the acknowledgement that I hadn't done anything wrong, and was cleared to get my visa again, would there be anything to go back to?

In those eighteen months things had gone so incredibly wrong that I could barely tell what I wanted. I began to convince myself that maybe it wasn't so bad after all and that maybe I wanted to live somewhere else—somewhere new. After all, I'd thrived time and again from going to new places.

During that time I went to stay with Dorian Yates in Spain. We had a great time partying and I began to feel truly relaxed for the first time in more than a year. I started to wonder whether I could make a real go of it in Europe and had a conversation with Ryan Deluca.

I enjoyed Spain but in a way I always knew I was trying to put a positive spin onto my life. I was trying desperately to imagine that life without the States could be a better life. I wanted it to be true so much so in my head it almost started to be true.

After the sheer despair of being denied the opportunity to present my case to the US embassy officer, I was on the ropes. The whole experience had wrecked me mentally and financially. It seemed like there was no light at the end of the tunnel.

We didn't give up though and we came back a third time. On this occasion we had managed to pull the right strings to get them to acknowledge that I had at very least the right to be taken seriously when I went to the embassy.

For the third time in a year, I was back at the grim great building that had been my downfall twice already. Once again,

I queued up and waited my turn, praying that I wasn't about to be subjected to the same painful fate of humiliation. Praying that I wouldn't be assigned the same woman who had crushed my hopes with glazed over eyes that offered not even a drop of sympathy or understanding.

As I was called to approach the bench I let out a sigh of relief at the sight of a new face. Maybe, it was just hard luck that I'd been given someone who didn't want to give me the time of day previously, or perhaps our persistence and pressuring had finally paid off—but this time I wasn't sent packing straight away. I was allowed to submit the file that we had spent more than a year slaving over.

When we finally hammered the open door at the embassy and got them to listen, I felt overjoyed. We were far from home and dry, but more than anything I was heartened that finally I had been listened to: that they were letting me present my side of the story to clear my name of wrongdoing.

The lawyer who had so royally screwed up my life in Boise was eventually de-barred and faced with punishment for his misdemeanours both to me and an array of others. But this hadn't mattered one iota up until now—the fact that he was guilty cleared me morally, but not legally. I was still fighting for that.

After perhaps the longest three weeks of my life, we got the news I had been yearning for and barely daring to hope. Having reviewed the case file we had submitted, they were lifting my ban on applying for a visa. I could now go back to square one and start over, free from the chains of my prior mistake.

We had won, or so it appeared on the surface. When the visa finally came through after another painful wait, the news was mixed. I had been given permission to return to the US but with an enormous drawback.

The visa application gave me just a year, rather than the three that is normally provided. And that's when it really struck me how hollow the victory was.

I travelled to the US for the first time in eighteen months and to begin with there was a surge of excitement at the prospect of seeing the Bodybuilding.com team and Boise once more. But, as I stepped off the plane, I felt a wave of fear come over me. The year I was afforded by my new visa meant I was never more than twelve months from having my life ripped apart again.

How could I put my life back together with that hanging over my head? It was a physical and emotional challenge that I couldn't put myself, Marika or my family through. The previous eighteen months had been too hard.

I used the time I had in the US to get a few bits in order. It was brilliant to be able to catch up with friends after so long but I always had that sensation that I was standing on the other side of a glass window looking in to this life. I could see it, but I couldn't touch it. It was fragile and fleeting.

Without the foundation of knowing that I couldn't be torn away from Boise again, I could never really live a happy life. I could only take solace from knowing how happy I had been before everything unravelled. It was better to have loved and lost, than to never have loved at all. I was broken hearted but trying to see the glass half full.

I attended Mr. Olympia on behalf of Bodybuilding.com which was a rather odd, yet enjoyable experience. The first time I went, as a fan-cum-journalist, I had been the one taking pictures and getting autographs. Now, I was in that same expo hall on the other side of the booth with fans crowding me for my autograph and picture. It was surreal but as always, meeting the people who had been inspired by our Video Trainer and book, *Body by Design*, was richly rewarding.

I was also allowed to shoot photographs on stage, the only journalist with that access. Robin Chang, who ran the event, was a friend by now and he afforded me the honour. And an honour it was—the adrenaline of being closer to the action than anybody else in the entire world is an unforgettable experience, no matter what else is going on elsewhere.

My visa gave me a year but I couldn't stay. It was never going to be the same while I had this guillotine hanging above my head. After a frank chat with Ryan we made the decision that we were going to do this properly. We weren't going to take half measures—as difficult as the fight had already been, I needed to secure a life in Boise. Not just a rolling window of opportunity that might be slammed shut if I slipped up.

We agreed that I would work elsewhere while I worked on getting a green card, for permanent residency in the States. It was the only way I could ever really return and build a life again. It was a difficult decision but we knew it was the only one that would ever work in the long run.

Where would I go in the meantime? I didn't have to kid myself any longer that I was content with not being in the US. I had a plan and although it might take many years to become a reality, I could enjoy the present without lying to myself about where I wanted to end up. I had hope, and that mattered immensely. I also had Ryan's support which kept me strong.

Spain appealed. It was a relatively easy option and the few weeks had been fun. I could see it working. Was it perfect? I wasn't sure but I had realised whilst working in the UK that I could work on a number of different projects wherever I wanted, as long as I had a laptop. If that was the case then there was nothing stopping me doing it somewhere with sun, beaches and good people.

I had run it by Ryan who saw the value from Bodybuilding. com's perspective because of the presence in Europe. I was ready to press 'Go', and Marika was geared up for the change too, when something extraordinary happened out of the blue.

After the long slog, and added complication of my exile from the US, *Body by Design* had launched. It was doing really well and I was incredibly proud of both completing it and its impact. Yet more stories flooded in on Bodyspace and by email as people used it to take them on their own personal path to transformation.

I knew it was being read around the world but I hadn't imagined quite how far word would travel. From Sydney to Russia and from Taiwan to Mumbai, there were people reading the book.

One of these people was somebody called Hrithik Roshan. Not that I had any idea at the time, but Hrithik was the world's leading star of Bollywood. And he was at the crossroads in his life, where injury had led him to lose his way a little. On the recommendation of a friend, he had read *Body by Design* and he not only wanted to follow its steps, he wanted me to help him do so.

When I was first told that his agents were trying to make contact, the gravity of the request hadn't really hit me. I was in limbo with the US and pretty set on a temporary home in Spain. Here was this offer, from somebody very far away, to come and train him. It was a curve ball that I slowly understood was a good opportunity.

With the States in my rear-view mirror, for the time being, I had a huge decision to make: Whether to go to Spain and play it relatively safe, continuing Nutrition by Design and the other projects I was working on, or go somewhere entirely new and meet the person behind the request.

Would I take the red pill or the blue pill? The training would last twelve weeks, so I figured, at worst I had nothing to lose but a couple of months. On that logic alone, I decided to go further down the rabbit hole. Nothing ventured, nothing gained. Next stop: Chhatrapati Shivaji International Airport.

14

Transforming the Indian Nation: A New Beginning

The moment I stepped out of the airport in Mumbai, I was instantly hit by a wall of energy, noise and life. Amid blaring rickshaw horns, cacophony of traffic snarls, aromas floating in the hot and thick air that changed from gasoline to spices at every turn, I—coming from the remoteness of Wales—could barely take in the onrush of sensations.

Everywhere I looked, there were smiles—welcoming me, encouraging me to come closer and see more of the Indian life. For the time being, I had very little opportunity to see or immerse myself in the culture.

I was there to do a job and as soon as I had landed and recuperated from the painfully long flight (I still don't like them!), I set to work with Hrithik.

I'd done a bit of research prior to the trip and I had gathered at least a passable understanding of his celebrity quotient. I knew of Bollywood but I couldn't say that I knew much more about it and certainly not who the stars of it were.

Hrithik had been a child star in Indian cinema, before starting a very successful career as an actor during the 2000s. He had played leading roles in box office breaking films including

Dhoom 2 and *Krrish*. He'd also received countless awards that recognised the formidable force he had become in Bollywood and his outstanding performances.

The film which he was preparing for at the time I met him was entitled *Krrish 3* and would go on to smash all sorts of records for Bollywood. He was already a huge star and this would propel him even further into stardom. I've never been intimidated by someone's celebrity status but it's safe to say that Hrithik was on a different scale of popularity for fans of Indian cinema.

When I met him, I was greeted by an incredibly humble and friendly person. He was honest and upfront with me. He wanted help and he was prepared to give me all the information and assistance I needed in order to get him out of his rut.

It became clear very quickly what the roots of the issue were. Hrithik was a tough guy and never shied away from experimenting with action-packed roles. Over time this had left him with a back injury (two slipped discs) that was debilitating if left untreated for long periods. He had been prescribed rest which had only made matters worse as his lack of activity seized up his body.

Hrithik was very open with me. He needed help and he knew that he had got into a cycle where he had lost control of his body. He was renowned for his physique but things had slipped away from him during his injury.

Apart from the spinal problem he also had trouble with his knee and he had been self medicating. He was suffering from Chondromalacia patellae, a condition where the underside of the patella in the knee cap suffers inflammation resulting in pain upon impact. As a result, Hrithik was being forced to walk sideways, downstairs to mitigate the discomfort.

Compounding both these challenges, Hrithik was emotionally eating on account of his injuries. It happens to lots of people, where the difficulties they are facing with their body or with the anxiety and stress of life lead them to eat as a form of comfort. The late night snacks and sedentary lifestyle were turning him from Adonis to slouch—and more importantly, leaving him depressed and feeling helpless.

Because Hrithik was so honest with me about the problems he was facing and was prepared to do whatever it took to make the changes ahead of filming, I knew he would complete a great transformation. He had the hallmarks of a well-motivated and hard-working individual and following reviews of his scans, x-rays, physical exams and blood reports that I had requested, I felt confident that given my understanding of injuries and rehabilitation, we could overcome his difficulties and demons.

At this point in my career, I had worked closely with hundreds of different individuals, all with unique needs and bodies. Over the course of several years, I had developed a process of training which I called Dramatic Transformation Principle. It was centred on weight training and assured stunning results. It was flexible enough to allow different people to adapt to the technique of the training.

Hrithik had a very small bone structure which meant that his joints would become inflamed easily. This presents a problem for the weight training and that meant we had to apply a lot of volume with intensity. When he was feeling strong and stable we would aim for compound movements with less intensity and less volume but increased loads of resistance. Doing so allowed us to keep Hrithik fit the whole time and let him maintain the momentum, which he relies upon so much.

He would question my directions but only so he could learn. Never would he doubt me. And I grew more proud each day with the focus and commitment he was showing.

I've heard every excuse in the book as to why people don't have the time to do their exercise or to eat enough meals each day. Having seen one of the hardest-working actors, who would work seven days a week for seven months without a break, do it—I just don't buy it from anyone else. If you want it, and Hrithik did, then you make time.

He would sometimes have to work night shifts but if he did then he would make up for his sleeping and rest time afterwards. And when it came to meals, he was brilliantly disciplined. One of the key factors in improving metabolism and giving the body a steady supply of good nutrition is upping the number of meals you eat each day. For Hrithik, who would spend hours and hours on sets, that was a real challenge. But he would do what he had to, asking the hundreds of people involved in the shoot to stop so he could eat. That was dedication—and he understood why it mattered.

I was delighted with both the progress Hrithik was making and how I felt about being in India. Truthfully, the first ten weeks were so busy that I barely had time to take in anything outside a mile radius of where I was based or in Hrithik's company. However, I was meeting people and it was them that really caught me by surprise—in a positive sense.

Indian people are, without a doubt, the happiest people I've met. Their courage, motivation and positivism are infectious. Life in India throws every manner of challenge at you in a new way every day—but they smile and face it with the same verve as each passing day. It was inspiring and wonderful to be around.

For me, off the back of the pain and disappointment in the States and then the UK, it was a breath of fresh air. It was impossible not to feel motivated when everyone around me was so infectiously well-spirited.

Hrithik powered through our training and though we had to carefully manage his small bone structure to avoid inflammation and injury, he was well ahead of schedule. From the moment I had met him I knew that despite his injuries he would be a great transformation, but I underestimated just quite how good.

Within eight weeks, he had already boiled down his body fat to a fraction of what it started at and his muscle was lean and in phenomenal shape. We had done a significant amount of cross-fit and functional work as part of his cardio which consisted of tyre flipping, sandbag carrying, kettle bell swings, hurdle jumping and Olympic lifting, and each and every technique paid off. Any possibility that *Krrish 3* might have to be cancelled had been dissipated and he looked ready to play the part of the superhero.

We were in Dubai at the time where we had just spent a week—celebrating the New Year's from Hrithik's balcony at the Address Hotel. We had access to the beach for early morning runs, great gym facilities for the intense workouts and clean food I had requested meal-for-meal from the hotel chef.

It brought a tear to my eye to see Hrithik's excitement as he performed sprint drills on the beach. It was the first time since he was a child that he had been able to run like that. There were many injuries he had been living with and how he overcame them all is commendable. I can't imagine another job giving me the satisfaction of moments like that.

Within nine weeks, he had reached his peak and he was beginning to lose focus. After a chat with Hrithik we decided that despite the original plan for twelve weeks we would finish up early because of the speed at which his body had changed. Certainly, his body was in part down to that but the commitment and drive shown by Hrithik was equally important.

During our time together, Hrithik and I had become good friends. We had bonded over our shared focus and ambition. He was a modest family man, who suffered none of the usual pitfalls of being a celebrity.

I had seen little of the real India but I was endeared by the people. I began to wonder whether I could spend more than the twelve weeks here. I had nothing really pulling me away and I had been able to continue writing articles while I was there.

Hrithik was as delighted by his transformation as I was and he offered me the chance to stay on working for him as his trainer. Hrithik's body was prone to slipping if he didn't maintain momentum so our partnership ought to continue, at least till the time the shooting was on. After some thought I accepted, drawn by his personality and excited to see what else India had in store for me.

Hrithik had a year's worth of filming for which he needed to be kept in peak physical condition. I wasn't ready to throw myself at India given how little I had seen of it. We settled on a three-month rolling basis which gave me the flexibility I needed to keep on my toes but also start exploring other opportunities in India.

At the same time, the long road to launching Nutrition by Design had come to fruition. This was a huge moment for me and Ruben. We had gone through more than fifteen different formulas to get the recipe right and then the painstaking process of organising production, supply and the accreditation we needed. And all of this was well before the prospect of getting them on the shelves was confirmed.

While it can be incredibly tough to launch a new product, particularly food, when there are thousands of others launching every single day, I knew that Nutrition by Design was a great product that solved a grave problem.

Having pitched the idea and the product to Bodybuilding. com, we got our first tentative orders: just a couple of cases to begin with. It was an incredibly tense moment and at that point it could have gone either way. Will we get the momentum that we need to ramp up production and make the economies of scale big enough to turn a profit? Or will the units trickle to a stop?

It was good news. Nutrition by Design generated favourable demand and within a week we were stocking more boxes, gradually crates and before we knew it we were doing steady business.

The challenge of getting accreditation continued to cause us trouble over the next few months. While I knew that if we could get it stocked in more countries we'd easily propel ourselves forward, the costs of getting approval to do so was wrapped in red tape that differed in complexity within every single country.

There were other things that we could never have known when we started out. For example, when we went into production, we discovered that the freeze-dried food would easily fit into the cups only when dry but when the food expanded, a larger cup would be a necessity. A simple problem and a seemingly obvious solution. But the problem was that the cup size we required didn't exist, so that meant building a new one from scratch. More cost and more time.

The difficulty and frustration did at times make me question whether it was worth it. It's rare that I would have the patience to stick with something so slow moving for the eighteen months it took from the idea to launch, which is why I'm grateful for Ruben's support. He kept me sane and made sure we hit the finish line with the energy we needed to make it work.

In India, the unbridled success of my video series and my book *Body by Design* gave me the confidence to start thinking about writing another book. It was an uphill struggle to convince people to switch from traditional Indian recipes to the usual and rather 'bland' food for a healthy living. My long stay in India had made me learn much about its people and their eating habits. After investing nearly four years into my first book, I once again began writing and working with my celebrity clients' chefs to distinguish the different properties of all the ingredients: spices, herbs and low-fat sauces. I researched more about their benefits and tried to understand the quantity of these ingredients the human body requires on a daily basis. I compiled an exhaustive list of vegetarian Indian dishes, to begin with, and soon delved into the meditative approach to training. I went into the finer details of taking on an AKA role model and many other subjects including: complete weight training, cardio, supplementation, daily meditation and nutrition program. What I had learned and applied on my successful Bollywood star clients had transformed them into incredible shape in a short span of time and I had to publish these findings to help other aspirants.

I knew I still wanted to do something big that would also stand the test of time. Not just something that would change the lives of those I could meet personally, but potentially an entire nation.

Indians are hard-working and motivated. I had gathered this from speaking to the people over the first few months of being in the country. They wanted so desperately to not only emulate the US and Europe when it came to sports and fitness but to lead the world with confidence and superior health condition. The individuals were full of passion and excitement but the gap was in the lack of education.

The comparison contrast with Australia is worth dwelling upon. I do mention, in the earlier chapters of this book, how the place is very sport enthusiastic while their work ethic is unmatched and as a result, they do extremely well as a small populated nation within the Olympics, Rugby, Cricket, Formula 1, boxing, tennis, etc.

In India, by contrast, 1.2 billion people struggle to notch a single medal at the Olympics and barely win the top spot in most world sports. The marked exception is cricket, the national game, for which the dedication and heritage of success pulls through.

This isn't a problem in itself—competitive sport is hardly the thing by which people should live and die. But it's symptomatic of the ground that India has to make up in understanding how to excel in health, fitness and sport.

For most of the 20th century, Indians neglected issues of fitness and health. They did not prioritise health over other social concerns. It is important to note that despite contradicting perceptions, the traditional Indian diet is good and wholesome. It is rarer to see a poor or even middle-income Indian suffering from obesity in the way that the Western world has become so plagued with. Excess was the only issue.

Times are changing and the number of people suffering from obesity in India has surged to an alarming ten per cent of the population. That is a miniscule amount compared to the UK or the US but it is growing far quicker. And at the core of that is the importing of Western food types, high in saturated fats and low in nutritional value.

Fast food is as likely to be on the plate of an Indian child as any other meal and the number of children suffering from weight problems are probably the most concerning factor. It has a direct and very real link to the biggest danger that India is facing—diabetes.

My understanding of the issues plaguing India didn't develop overnight but I was learning about the opportunities people in India hadn't well explored to improve their knowledge of health and fitness. It was exciting to realise the possibilities and I wanted to give my best to the mission I had set out on.

While I was in exile in Wales, I'd spent quite a bit of time with a friend called Neil Hill. I knew Neil through Flex Lewis, as they'd been working together (Neil was Flex's trainer) for nearly a decade. We had become great friends since the Dorian-Flex shoot in Birmingham and he had even stayed at my place in Boise for a while as I had asked him prepare Marika for the New York Pro Bodybuilding Show a couple of years earlier.

He was without a doubt the finest trainer I'd ever met and he was an inspiration to be around. He was also much fun and a pool of knowledge. We learned a lot from one another while we trained and we had hung out in his amazingly beautiful hometown of Tenby, Wales.

We talked in depth about our training principles—mine being DTP and his Y3T—a training system that worked over a three-week cycle by targeting the entire muscle fibre population. There was a great deal of common ground and we soon realised the two were complementary, offering different benefits that could be adapted for clients.

Around the time that I had finished Hrithik's first transformation, things went crazy. The photographs of the transformation were plastered across national newspapers, TV news bulletins, magazines and the Internet. It was a sensation and it wasn't hard to see why. Hrithik was already a big celebrity and to see the shape he had gotten in, and what he'd beaten his way back from, was incredible. He was living the superhero body that his upcoming film needed.

The flip side (if I may call it) of this was that I shot from obscurity to big news in India. The offers and invitations came flooding in from other actors and people from across the subcontinent. It was almost impossible to keep up, but the reality was that with my exclusivity to Hrithik, I was off the table.

I wanted to help though—this was a huge moment. The energy and excitement inspired by Hrithik's transformation couldn't be left to slip. I phoned Neil and talked to him about my own experiences. How I'd come to India with my expectations of a short stay and grown to admire the people. And I explained to him the project I was working on—the sort that only comes along once.

Surprisingly, Neil was up for it. He's the most down to earth person you'll meet so I don't think it was the chance to work with celebrities here that swung it. After all, neither of us was really fanatic about Bollywood! He was charmed by the story of the gap that I wanted to bridge and we set about considering a way to fill it.

Neil and I decided to meet and discuss the challenges and the possible opportunities.

The plans weren't enormous but they were groundbreaking for India. We decided to couple my training philosophy with Neil's as part of a bigger and more powerful brand. In turn, we would do the one thing I had always struggled to do before—to train others in the skills that we had learned and make them competent enough to help others. Our ideas would be at the heart but through education and delegation, we could reach not just hundreds but thousands and touch millions. When you're trying to change a country of more than a billion people, we had to think this big.

The concept we came up with, in its basic form, was an initial training course that would be given to a group of master trainers who could then educate and certify other trainers. The level of detail and deep understanding we imparted meant that our most trusted circle of students would be able to go and spread the same principles of education. We did not leave any stone unturned in terms of ensuring the rigour was carried forward without serious lapses along the way.

Neil and I would pull trainers from the UK, the US and elsewhere and provide them with the highest skills needed to plug the gap of demand that we had uncovered in India. By carefully building up a network of the elite we could then match up the clients, who were coming thick and fast through the publicity surrounding Hrithik's transformation, and discuss the training philosophies and techniques sorely needed in India.

The process was self-perpetuating. By bringing Neil on board, our capacity was already doubled and the success experienced with each client would in turn bring in more, as well as greater awareness of the importance of health and fitness in the country as a whole. As our network grew, we were then confident to provide trainers to further clients, celebrity and otherwise. And so, the circle continued to expand.

One of these individuals was a friend named Lloyd Stephens. Lloyd had been inspired by the DTP principles after watching my Bodybuilding.com video series and then reading my book. Every day, I get innumerable messages asking for my support or simply thanking me and Bodybuilding.com for giving them the power to transform their lives.

Lloyd's message stuck out and we struck up a relationship by email. I was impressed by his knowledge and understanding and his thirst for more. His passion and attention to detail in his own amazingly inspiring physical transformation told me just what a bright talent he was and when we started I was determined that we would give him an opportunity to prove himself.

At the time, he was running a jet-ski business in Bournemouth in the UK but wanted to make the jump to become a full-time personal trainer. These things can't be learned instantly but with the base of education he already had and our course, he showed he had what it took. I decided he had the attitude and the skills to take it to the next level and he became one of the first trainers we brought over to India to work with our clients. He had floored us enough to wear the badge of our training principles.

And not just any client. Lloyd worked with Bollywood actor Ranveer Singh who had risen to fame for his starring roles in films including *Ram-Leela* where he played a character based upon Romeo, from *Romeo and Juliet*. It was a colossal opportunity for Lloyd and he rose to the challenge proving our faith in him was well founded.

We continued to expand the programme, ensuring the level of rigour remained at its absolute peak. We've trained more than 1,800 trainers in the principles of DTP and Y3T. We have also trained as many as 800 trainers worldwide outside of India as well. Our schedules are usually very busy but we occasionally steal a few days to educate and certify Personal Trainers.

I have been looking to overcome one of the greatest challenges that bodybuilding in India face, which is where they can get the supplements needed to transform quickly and effectively. Intake of supplements does not lead to drastic changes in your body, they make it significantly easier for you to get the amount of nutrition you would otherwise have to find in regular meals. Basically, they are there to improve your health, performance and recovery by providing the amounts of nutrients impossible to get from food.

When you're trying to plug six meals into your day, there could be a few hiccups because a lot of people find it physically difficult to eat that much food. Supplements are not a shortcut (that's a misconception many fall prey to), they're exactly what their name implies—supplements to your diet—a boost and a way to accurately ensure you're getting your protein and other nutrition without incessant delays or lapses.

What India is still grappling with is the scarcity in the availability of genuine high-grade supplements. The industry is still maturing and part of the roadblock is the prevalence of red tapes that comes in the way of introducing these products.

For years, I had been mixing certain single ingredients in efficacious dosages to make my own formula because there were a lot of unwanted ingredients within the 'pre-packaged' supplements' category available in the market. As it became harder to source 'Patented' ingredients over 'Generic' ingredients and purchase supplements that improved health as well as performance, I decided to speak with some of the world's best scientists, formulators and doctors to share my views. Over months of Skype conversations, conference calls and in-person meetings, I was lucky enough to encourage them into joining me to develop a supplement company the world hadn't seen before. We set about testing natural, pure, innovative, patented, and pharmaceutical grade ingredients over a two-year period before our possible public release to ensure there was no loophole, and I was the primary guinea pig.

I was tested under every environment imaginable. Firstly, I decided to stay away from the gym for four months as I prepared for a triathlon to verify the efficacy of the ingredients under extreme endurance conditions such as: swimming, running and cycling. Within shorter distances, I explored the benefits of these supplements in areas of: hydration, mineral balance, electrolyte function, lactic acid buffering and energy regulation. Rigorous training helped a great deal and I managed

188 / The Transformer

to finish my first ever triathlon within the top 80 from over 230 competitors. Despite the trouble I faced swimming one length of a pool only four months earlier, I was extremely happy with my progress.

Immediately after the triathlon, I took on another challenge to test more ingredients under a contrasting environment. My goal was to try and put on 15Ibs of lean muscle tissue in twelve weeks. I wanted to have this documented daily, for a video series, to be published on *Bodybuilding.com*. The website attracts hundreds of thousands of unique visitors per day, so I thought shooting in Mumbai would draw in more viewers and Indians would learn about transforming their bodies with local foods, supplements and gym equipments.

I managed to supersede my expectations yet again by adding 20lbs of lean muscle onto my frame. With such concrete results, things started looking extremely positive as we closed in on several innovative ingredients to launch for the public.

Several months later, we launched KAGED MUSCLE worldwide, sold exclusively through Bodybuilding.com. In the space of eight months, KAGED MUSCLE supplements climbed from the 450th rank to number 14 in the world. We have already received the highest ratings globally and continue to break barriers and records. I couldn't be happier to be working with a team consisting of the world's greatest formulators, manufacturers, doctors, MD's, PhD's and Naturopathic Physicians to produce something valuable for health-conscious people.

My work with Hrithik had continued, on the rolling three-month basis, during the course of his filming. It meant I was on the road from location to location at the drop of a hat. From Jordan to Hyderabad and Mumbai to Dubai—it was a rollercoaster that kept me hanging on. You could never predict what Hrithik's schedule would be and delays were part of the reality of working with him. You just got on with it, knowing well how important it was to him—he never let me down and his level of commitment was praiseworthy.

It was necessary that I remained by his side throughout the filming simply because I could never predict when his injury might flare up. And the film couldn't afford to miss a day when there are hundreds of other people behind the same project and are working day in day out on the sets.

One problem he consistently faced was on long haul flights or long drives navigating the tough roads of India. The lack of motion would cause his back to seize up and leave him in agony. We developed a method of overcoming this by putting two tennis balls in a sock and placing them in a way that enabled him to gently massage his back during his travels. The simple motion and pressure placed on his spine he was temporarily alleviated of pain to ensure his core remained strong and he, fit and healthy.

The nature of the work with Hrithik and other clients since, including John Abraham and Mahesh Babu, meant that even over the course of more than three years, I'm still yet to really see much of India. I'm usually confined to hotels and airports for a large amount of the time—those are two places I'm very familiar with now!

The one place where I did get to know India and its people was the gym. Wherever I go I have to find the time to workout—it remains my therapy and my opportunity to find myself. I'm never happier than when I'm pounding those last few reps and shredding my muscles to failure.

In India, the gyms have a number of differences. Perhaps, the most frustrating for me is their attitude toward professionals like myself. There's little respect for our industry and the attitude of lots of gym owners is to see individuals like me as a potential threat to their business. They wrongly presume that I'm there to poach their clients. The reality is I'm desperate to do what I love and get my training sessions in at a decent gym.

In addition to this, there really is a dearth of gyms of the quality and standard that you need in order to really unlock people's potential. Poor equipment is a start, without a decent set of machines the chances of injury increase and the efficiency of exercise decrease significantly. But the cleanliness, standard of training, professionalism and range of equipment are often found wanting as well.

The net impact is that the millions who have the motivation and the will are left high and dry, unable to fulfil their ambitions. Along with education, it is probably the biggest stumbling block for India's fitness and health industry.

Setting up gyms for India with the promise of transformation was the next big step. I couldn't have put my name to a product without running through the pros and cons. I wanted to do it the right away and in right time. From my experience in Australia I knew that unless I was certain that the Gethin name was being done justice, I would never consider delegating the skills to a gym franchise.

With careful planning and support from others, including my good friend, manager and now business partner Jag Chima, we're finally at an exciting stage where our dream is all set to take wings. The intention is to launch a Gethin Gym in Chennai and Hyderabad by early 2016. The motive is to bring the finest equipment and infrastructure that you will ever find inside a fitness centre.

As for the gyms, the whole experience will be on a par with that I would provide myself—an elite gym range centrally controlled by Jag and myself and managed by a team of experts and professionals. We intend to build a successful business, not by simply signing up people and then pushing them out of the door like so many other existing gyms, but by customer loyalty that recognises the quality of what is on offer.

There's pressure on me, which is why I talk about it in such strict terms. It is not a casual affair; the key is to ensure we run it properly and grow fast enough to meet all the expectations and demands in order to ride the crest of the wave we initiated by training Hrithik and others. In the process, we cannot afford to either over stretch or dilute the quality and standard I insist upon at all times. It has to be done right or not at all. Thankfully, we've got the right people on board to make that the case. People as passionate as us want to help people change their lives, not simply run a business. I have spent over a year with Jag, writing manuals for the Gethin Gyms franchise, conceptualising architectural designs, developing training principles, programmes and schedules, choosing the world's finest equipment manufactures and interviewing potential staff members.

I've continued to contribute articles to publications around the world, including *Men's Health* in India for my column, 'Mind Over Muscle'. My longer-term ambition is to land a newspaper column and a radio show to further increase the number of readers and the people we want to reach.

It's true that I derive a sense of accomplishment in contributing toward every transformation through multiple platforms—my published books, online training, magazine columns, video series, seminars, DTP certifications, supplements, and now gyms—my quest for other means to communicate with people to help them on their journey through motivation, education and inspiration ceases to end.

I had conceptualised an idea for a comic character named Kaged Muscle who would inspire people to take better care of themselves by building strength, confidence and superhero-like muscles in the gym, and of course would also display the occasional physical heroism by beating up villains to save the day. Fortunately, the CEO of a popular comics publishing company liked my idea and we began building upon a detailed storyboard. After rounds of editorial discussions and finalising design elements and sketches, we came out with a handsomely packaged graphic novel.

We set to work and enjoyed an amazing process over nine months to complete what is now a bestselling graphic novel. The reviews have been favourable and the sales have gone worldwide ever since. I will soon be making my first ever appearance at the Comic Con convention in Mumbai end of 2015. My commitment to the gym, the food and supplements I feed myself give me the strength and energy to execute my plans and strive for more.

To transform the mentality of a nation, I had to think out of the box and find a way to reach them in every space of their lives. It makes for a schedule that relies upon me busting a gut to keep going with no moments wasted. The success of my motivational and educational morning seminars along with several afternoon practical workshops has taken me across the US, Australia, UAE, India and the UK. Hosting these seminars is immensely satisfying; I treat them like a live performance by a musical artist who sings with a greater zeal than the last offering. There's nothing more rewarding than reading various testimonials and learning people's positive reaction on benefitting from these seminars and workshops. When I hear, prior to one of my seminars, that many people have flown in from far away countries or have travelled many hours to attend it makes me very nervous but the pressure I feel is good because it forces me to reach above my means.

Ultimately, my hope and plan was always to return to Boise and the US. I had been working hard to obtain green cards for Marika and myself that would allow us to be residents for good. As I write, I have recently obtained these green cards and now spend my time between two residences within Cardiff, Wales and Boise, Idaho. I will be spending at least half of the year in the US while the rest of the time is spent travelling for work, working from my apartment in Cardiff and spending time with my family in Mid Wales.

My sister gave birth to the most beautiful little girl in 2013—my niece, Alys. I have never wanted children of my own but Alys has become close to my heart. She is cute, smart (already very good at speaking two languages. She is only two years old), funny, independent, troublesome (in a fun way), and makes me happier than anything. My beautiful little niece has turned my bad days into good; if only she could stay this age forever, I'd never feel unhappy.

During early 2015, I put my body and mind through another challenge of getting in top physical condition in as little as four weeks. I did this for several reasons—to prove to naysayers that it could be done, to further test my KAGED MUSCLE single-form ingredients and supplement formulations, because I was proud of the fact that I could film this daily video series from my home country in Wales. As I have argued before, with every transformation, I learn and discover so much about myself that I am able to channelise the benefits into other areas of my life to make another positive progression and impact.

For four weeks within Cardiff, a camera crew followed me every single day as they documented my transformation. The end result was a video series called 4Weeks2Shred and published on www.KAGEDMUSCLE.com that had witnessed me slash my body fat in half, over four weeks. I also encountered my first ever serious injury at the gym. During the filming of the very first episode, I tore my lat—a muscle within the upper outer back. I didn't tell my KAGED MUSCLE team, the film crew or family. I didn't want the concern from others to slow me down. I knew they would have probably encouraged me to postpone the shoot. The injury was not a deterrent; on the contrary, I used this as a fuel to the challenge. I went public with pictures that displayed a very black and blue lat muscle upon the time of publication. This further proved that the mind could be a powerful tool to succeed under adverse conditions. I have since recovered fully with a few adjustments to my training regime. When 4Weeks2Shred went live, it garnered much attention. My effort silenced the naysayers.

In the meantime, I have incredibly exciting challenges from all fronts upon my hands. The distance travelled in the last sixteen years since I discovered the power of transformation has been exhilarating. Barring the pain of my visa fiasco, I've barely had a second to reflect upon what a journey it has been.

Bodybuilding flourished from a hobby to my career; an all-pervasive force in my life and ever increasing in scope and method. Each plateau I reached was overcome through mental and physical transformation that pushed me into the unknown.

I have evolved as a person, learning new skills and new passions whilst meeting incredible people. However, for all the changes I have made and encouraged others to make, I am still that curious kid from the farm Wales who wants to go explore in the woods. I want to wake up each day with a challenge that seems beyond me and probably is.

I continue to have end goals—just as I do with my transformations. They are what keep me focused and ensure

I'm accountable to my efforts. Our plans for India are without a doubt the most ambitious and all-encompassing yet.

My battle to return 'home' to the US is now complete. My heart remains in Boise and my green card has secured my future there and will allow me to continue to do everything I love: working with KAGED MUSCLE and Bodybuilding.com while striving to improve the lives of millions in India, the US, the UK, and all over the world. Nothing has ever diminished my desire to rebuild my life and overcome even greater hurdles in the process.

In the end though, the journey is what matters. Whether I'm trying to get in shape for the Natural World Bodybuilding Championships or launching a supplement line. Whether I'm creating a video series or purchasing a gym. Whether I'm reporting on Mr. Olympia via webcast or sitting in a coffee shop writing a book. Whether I am certifying personal trainers or launching a Gym franchise. Whether I'm working on a graphic novel or conducting seminars, I need to be enjoying it all, because that's the fuel to move forward. Enjoy the journey and you'll have few regrets. Success will come and leave but you'll look fondly upon both its arrival and departure. The trick is neither to be too overjoyed when it falls on your lap, nor be crestfallen at its betrayal.

Wherever my career takes me, and I hope it will take me just as far in the next sixteen years as the last, there's little doubt that I'll continue to be at my most content in the gym. That's where my transformation began and it's where I find myself, whether I'm in Venice or on a cruise liner, Idaho or Mumbai, Sydney or Cardiff, Builth Wells or in one of the many gyms I have visited while travelling. The gym is a place dear to my heart; it boosts my confidence, gives me hope, helps me understand and come closer to my inner being.

At the end of a day of calls, meetings, seminars, formulations, training sessions, filming, writing, public speaking, photography… nothing sets you free like the solitude of putting the headphones on and hitting the weights—the burn, the relief and the rush of your inner being, not just physically but mentally too. In life, as in the gym, never stand still and never lose momentum. You'll always be moving in the right direction. Every single transformation I have undergone, it has propelled me further in life to tap opportunities, to become more motivated, focused and innovative. I will continue to challenge myself physically every year to achieve yet another record-breaking transformation. Spiritually and mentally, the after-effects are limitless, surprising, enlightening and rewarding. If you want to charge yourself up with life's batteries every day, hit the gym, ride your bike, go for a morning walk, play a game of football, join a gym class, and reward your body with healthy food and natural high-grade supplements. If you want life to love you, you have to love yourself— be compassionate and find a new reason, a purpose each day to love your life.

Find muscular failure in the gym to discover your real limits and potential outside its confines. Turn your weakness into a weapon. Transform impossibilities into opportunities. Control your environment and never let the latter control you.

Do what you fear, and don't fear what you do.

Acknowledgements

This book would never have surfaced without the upbringing, work ethic, independence, advice and support from my parents. Thanks for always being there for me.

A big thank you to the readers of my books, the viewers of my video series, attendees of my seminars, the loyal supporters of my supplements, and every single person who comments or writes a testimonial on my social networking websites. Your comments and suggestions fill me with a limitless supply of motivation and purpose to always deliver more and inspire more. Thank you for always listening, watching, viewing and showing up—I promise to never let you down.

My highest appreciation goes to Ajay Mago and Dipa Chaudhuri of Om Books International for believing in me and providing me the platform to share the values of health and fitness with readers across the globe. You have transformed thousands of lives by publishing my previous book—*Bollywood Body by Design*—and would do so once again by publishing *The Transformer*, my memoir. Ipshita Mitra, thank you so very much for being such an able ally. We all make a great team! Thank you for accepting me as a team player.

Christopher Westgarth, you have been an invaluable pillar of strength in giving structure to my thoughts and expressing them coherently through the pages of this book. Thank you for your clear translation, Chris.